MERRY'S BOOK

OF

BIRDS.

EDITED BY

UNCLE MERRY.

NEW-YORK:
H. DAYTON, No. 36 HOWARD STREET.
INDIANAPOLIS, IND.: ASHER & CO.
1860.

VINCENT L. DILL, STEREOTYPER,
128 Fulton Street.

CONTENTS.

ENGRAVINGS.

PREFACE.

I REMEMBER well, that I once thought I could catch any bird, if I could only sprinkle a little salt on his tail. I did not stop to inquire what good the salt would do. I took it for granted, either that the bird could not fly while it was there, or that the salt would make him so tame, that he would hop into my hand at once. How many times I tried the experiment, but I never succeeded in catching the bird. Still, I could not positively say that the plan would not work, I never could get near enough to put the salt in the right place; so that the way is still open for any who wish it, to try the experiment for themselves. If any one should succeed, I hope he will lose no time in reporting the case to me, with all the particulars, that I may use it in my next edition, or perhaps in another volume on Birds; for I would like exceedingly to show to all the young folks how birds can be charmed, and made familiar, without being trapped and caged, or deprived of the free use of all their powers.

In the mean time, I have brought together here, a few specimens of the bird family, that have been charmed on to the paper for me, by an art peculiar to the engraver, who first *draws* them without touching or alarming them, and then *cuts* them without drawing blood, or disturbing a feather, and then presses them, and holds them fast, without at all interfering with their natural liberty. In accomplishing all this, he uses, I am told, a kind of salt, called *attic salt*, of which his profession has the monopoly — at least, they monopolize that peculiar variety which is needful to do this work—none of it is ever found in market for sale. So that that could not have been the kind which I was told to use.

This book is not a cage, but a tree, or a garden ; where the birds play " hide and seek " among the leaves. And I cordially invite my young friends, one and all, to enter it when they please, examine the birds, handle them, talk with them, and learn all they can about them.

They will be sure to find it a pleasant and a profitable study. And it will help them to know something about the birds they see in the forests and the fields, their habits of life, and how they should be treated. Do you know that there is such a thing as *cultivating birds*, without shutting them up in cages, or coops. You can, if you will, make acquaintance with many kinds of birds and get them acquainted with you, so that they will not be afraid when you approach them, they will often come to meet you, as you call them, or go out to feed them. Even many of the wild birds have been tamed to this extent, and gradually domesticated, so as to remain about the ponds, or lakes, to which they have been drawn, and even to make companions of the tame fowls in the barn yard. To secure this kind of intercourse and acquaintance, you must be careful never to alarm the birds, you must keep guns out of their way, and never attempt to catch them. Begin by supplying them with the food they like, in their own way. They will soon learn who provides it and wait for his coming, and, in their eagerness to get it, will approach you as you go to the place where you leave it. Little by little, they will learn that you are a friend, and not an enemy. And this is all you wish to teach them: they will trust you, as long as you show that you have no designs upon their liberty.

Merry's Book of Birds.

SWALLOWS.

WE were going to say, that every body is acquainted with the swallow, but in fact, there are few who know, that there are four kinds of swallow, perfectly distinct in plumage and habits. There is the sand-martin, who excavates his nests in a sand-bank; the twittering blue-bodied swallow, who builds in our chimneys, the house martin, who nestles in the upper angle of a window, or under the jutting roof; and the long-winged, active swifts, known by their dark plumage, and their circling, in calm evenings, at a great height. They all live upon insects. The chimney swallow is a perfect pattern of maternal affection : from morning to night, during the whole summer, she is continually skimming close to the ground, hunting for flies for her young brood. Bewich gives an amusing account of a swallow that had become quite attached to the children by whom he was reared. They used to go out to the fields together, the bird being permitted to fly wherever he wished ; but he kept always circling above them wherever they went. When one of the children caught a fly, he called the swallow, with a whistle, when it immediately descended, and perched on the hand of the child, who had the fly prepared for him.

Swallows, when they return from warm climates, usually occupy the nests they left the fall before, if they can find them. Once, upon a time, a sparrow who was too lazy to make a nest for herself, had occupied a swallow's nest, laid her eggs, and begun to sit upon them, when the owner appeared, The swallow tried every way she could think of to make the sparrow give up the nest ; but no, she was determined, like some other fraudulent beings, to keep what she had got. At last the swallow flew away for a little while, and then returned, accompanied by many other swallows, each with a little well-tempered mortar in his bill, with which they closed up the opening of the nest, and left the poor sparrow to perish by suffocation, or hunger, or both.

This story, though almost incredible, is said by naturalists to be true.

When I see boys or grown-up men amusing themselves with shooting swallows, I am willing to believe that they do not think of the misery which they are causing. To kill a swallow flying, may be a very difficult thing ; and shooting of this kind may be thought very good practice : but the Creator did not make swallows that they might be put to death for amusement or for practice.

Some birds do a great deal of harm to our fields and gardens ; and to destroy them seems to be a matter of self-defence ; but the poor swallow does us no harm at all : there is reason to think that he is sent to do us good. When he is darting through the air, and wheeling round and round so swiftly that the eye can hardly follow him, he is catching flies, which are intended to be his food. Many thousands and millions of flies are destroyed in this way : and if they were all suffered to live, they would in time cover the earth ; and we should be as badly off as the Egyptians, when God sent upon them the plague of flies and other insects. We ought to feel much obliged to the swallows for lessening the number of these troublesome guests.

We should also remember, that the swallows come to our houses and barns to build their nests. They set about this very soon after their arrival ; and when their young ones are strong enough to fly, they all leave the country. It is hardly possible, therefore, to kill a swallow, without robbing some little birds of a father or a mother. The female swallow leaves her nest on a summer's evening, and fills her beak with flies. But she does not catch them only for herself: she has some young children at home, and she is thinking of them all the time that she is gliding through the air after her prey.

When she is returning to her nest with her mouth full of food, she is suddenly struck with a shot, and down she drops to the ground, bleeding and dead.

This may be sport for the boys, but I call it downright cruelty and robbery to the birdlings in the nest waiting for the Mother bird to come home and feed them, as she has been used to do.

The birds love *their* home and children, and are as earnest and devoted to them as we are; and I hope none who read this this book will ever be guilty of killing one of these little ones.

MY BIRD-CAGE.

I HAVE always been fond of studying the habits of the bird race, and have already indulged myself by appearing under the title of Minnie, in "Birds at Home." Now my birds are as much at *home* in their cage, as the free and unimprisoned songster in the wood. They were born and bred in a store, where feathered companions, of all sorts, colors, and countries, vied with them in making the greatest noise possible. To them the green, shady forest with its tall, waving trees and its rustling leaves, is unknown; the sparkling brook, in which they might dip their feathers, or drink refreshing drops, is tc them represented by a long tin basin, with water in it, bought for so much a pail ; and their food, instead of being sought and found by them, is daily supplied by the hand of their mistress. Yet there is an instinctive love for green branches and fresh earth, that shows itself in birds who, for generations back, have been the inhabitants of cages. I bought a plant, at the flower-market, with long, slender limbs, and full of flowers; and, setting it within their large cage, I withdrew a little to watch the effect of it. For a moment they all remained transfixed : then, one by one, they gradually approached the unknown object, and finally all lodged in its branches, investigating every leaf and flower, dancing up and down, picking in the earth, or singing with delight at their new, but natural position.

I have a pair of Canaries, of a pale yellow, both great pets : and knowing that they are a very presuming couple, the first drink from the fresh water, the first plunge into the bath, the largest seed, and the first bite at the sugar, are claimed by them ; and woe to any other hungry little fellow who dares approach them when thus employed !—he is liable to a sharp peck, and to any quantity of grimaces and threatenings. The life of the male is quite a little romance in itself. He is a remarkably dignified bird, moving with stateliness along the perches, looking daggers at the other birds who happen to touch him, and never unbending except to me ; but me he kisses regularly every day, when I go to wish them all good morning, and will come out of his cage to me at any moment. I know that this is half because he thinks there is a piece of sugar in perspective, but the other half is love for me ; for others might offer him a whole sugar-loaf, or a plantation of sugar cane, and they could not prevail upon him to accept, or even look at their bribes. I bought him first, and had him alone for a month or so ; and then fearing he was lonely, I bought a lovely, bright-eyed little wife for him, and expected he would be very happy. Would you believe it ?—for weeks he would take no notice of her, except to peck her when she came and sat by him, chirping her friendship, in a soft sweet voice, that, to look at him, you would have thought was a peacock screaming, or a pencil squeaking on a slate. Finally, however, he seemed to begin to appreciate her, and as one by one new birds began to arrive in the cage, he allowed her to be more with him, and began to whisper to her, now and then. Whether he was telling her that he liked her better, or merely making remarks against the new comers, I do not know.

About a month ago, I opened the cage-door, as usual, and out came the pair, to take their morning exercise to look for sugar that we would hide, or to pick up crumbs of bread and cake under the breakfast-table. I never saw a tamer or more interesting little bird than Madam Canary. She had a hundred amusing ways peculiar to herself. She would play hide with a piece of sugar, screaming aloud with delight when she found it in a great curl of my brother's hair, run after it along the floor as fast as we could roll it, or fly into some corner, and then call us in a loud voice to find her. I was beginning to think of teaching her to wheel a wheel-barrow, or fire a miniature cannon, when her little lamp of life was rudely blown out, and poor gentleman Canary was a widower! I was going out of the room in a hurry, to shut the door before the bird could follow me. I was either too quick or not quick enough; for the spirited Mrs. Canary was determined to go with me, and the door struck her, not hard, but just enough to snap her frail little life, and without a word, she fell dead at my feet. We all stood flabbergasted for a moment; then my brother picked her up, and I ran out of the room. Fifteen minutes had not passed away, when I heard my name called, and with red eyes, (I am not ashamed to admit that I cried somewhat,) I came to see what was wanted. In the cage was a bird so like the little one I had just killed, that for a moment I was startled; but it was only for a moment, for, as I approached the cage, she flew from instead of towards me, and I saw that the place of the bird had been made good, but not the affection or manner. The widower (Socrates) will have nothing to say to her, and she proves a perfect Xantippe toward him, doing all in her power to make his life uncomfortable. Within a day or two, I have separated them, and he is now rather more at peace, though he has looked

THE STORK.

IN form, the stork and the ibis, the sacred bird of the Egyptians, resemble each other. They both have legs like a crane—so slender, as to seem unable to sustain the large body of the bird. The ibis is black. The white stork is from three and a half to four feet in height, including the neck. Because of the slight, long legs, it walks very slowly, and with measured steps, like a soldier marching. Its flight is wonderful, being very long continued, and in the higher regions of the air.

Storks are birds of passage. They live in the deserts of Africa and Arabia, in the winter season. In summer they return to the cool climates, where they build their nests on old towers and belfries, and chimneys of the highest houses, and tall, dead trees. Both ibis and stork feed on reptiles, such as serpents, lizards, toads, etc., and in marshy tracts, the people fix a cart wheel by the center, to a long pole, and the storks rarely fail to build there. It seems to suit them admirably ; and for years the faithful pairs return—this they all do, to their nests, inhabiting them for many years. The eggs are never less than two, and seldom exceed four.

The Bible says, " As for the stork, the fir-tree is her house." Upon the fields between Cana and Nazareth, they were in such numbers, that the ground was whitened by them ; and in their flight they darkened the air like great clouds. The stork "knoweth her appointed time;" this is the time for passing from one land to another. A fortnight pre-

THE IBIS.

vious to this, they collect from all the country around, and appear to be in council, and are said by some to determine the exact time of departure, and place of future abode. At an amazing height they soar—the Bible says, "in the heaven."

Cuvier says, "that in mummies of the ibis there have been found undigested parts of skin and scales of serpents."

Many, of both ibis and stork, are in and around Constantinople, and are useful, because they feed on vermin, and garbage of the shambles, and refuse of the houses. The Turks esteem these birds highly. The tall, round pillars of the towers on the mosques of Bagdad are *without* a cone on the top, differing in this from the mosques of Constantinople. On the former the storks delight to build, and the cylindrical nest of great sticks makes a *capital* (literally), especially when the stork's head is out for a finish.

In Holland and Germany the stork is universally protected. Boxes are built for them on the tops of houses; and it is regarded as an excellent omen when a stork builds upon a man's house. They are easily tamed, and have been tamed to remain in gardens, where they destroy the reptiles. It is a sober, stately bird, with its almost solemn way of walking; but a writer has said that one or two had been known to join the play of children who frequented the grounds daily. One of these was the game of "*tag*," and when the bird was touched with tag, like the children, it would make its pipe-stem legs fly about merrily, in a regular run.

HUMMING-BIRDS.

A GENTLEMAN who made a voyage up the river Amazon, and who afterwards published an account of his travels in that part of the country through which this noble stream flows, gives some interesting particulars respecting the humming-birds he saw. There are varieties of this bird there, which are never seen among us. They are much more abundant, too, in that country, than they are here. "Wherever," says this writer, "a creeping vine opens its fragrant cluster, or wherever a tree-flower blooms, these little things may be seen. In the garden or in the woods, over the water, everywhere, they are darting about, of all sizes—from one that might easily be mistaken for a different variety of bird, to the Hermit, whose body is not half the size of the bees buzzing about the same sweets. The blossoms of the inga-tree bring them in great num bers. Sometimes they are seen chasing each other in sport, with such a rapidity of flight, and with such a winding path, that the eye is puzzled to follow them. Again, circling round and round, they rise high in mid air, then dart off, like light, to some distant object. Perched upon a little limb, they smooth their plumes, and seem to delight in their dazzling hues ; then, starting off leisurely, they skim along, stopping a moment, perhaps, just to kiss the flowerets. Often two meet in the air, and furiously fight, their crests and the feathers upon their throats all erected and blazing, and altogether pictures of the most violent rage. Several times we saw them battling with large black bees, who frequent the same flowers, and may be supposed often to interfere provokingly. Like lightning, our little heroes would come down, but the coat of shining mail would ward their furious strokes ; again and again would they renew the attack, until their anger had expended itself, or until the bee, once roused, had put forth powers that drove the invader from the field. A boy in the city several times brought us humming-birds, alive, in a glass cage. He had brought them down while, standing motionless in the air they rifled the flowers, by balls of clay thrown from a hollowed tube.

Wilson says that the only note of the humming-bird is a chirp, not much louder than that of a cricket or grasshopper. It is generally uttered while the bird is passing from flower to flower, or when he is engaged in a fight with some one of his neighbors. "I have seen the humming-bird attack, and, for a few moments, worry a king-bird," says the same writer, "I have also seen him, in his turn, assaulted by a humble bee, which he soon put to flight. He is one of those few birds that are universally beloved."

Formerly humming-birds were supposed to live entirely on the honey they collected from the flowers. But it is now certain that they feed, in part at least, on insects. Indeed, I have seen the little fellows engaged in fly-catching, and it seemed to be very pretty sport for them. Perhaps their errand to the flowers has as much to do with the capture of insects they find there, as with the honey at the bottom of the corolla. I think it quite likely, in fact, though I do not agree with those who tell us, that the humming-bird eats insects only, and that he has nothing to do with honey; for it is found, that, when the bird is confined for a while in the house, until he becomes hungry, he eats honey and sugar with a good relish.

There are seventy kinds of humming-birds, nearly all of them natives of America; yet only one kind visits the United States, where it is well known, as it frequents the gardens, and sips the hoı ey from the honey-suckle and other plants, like the hive and humble bee. It is several times larger than the latter, but flies so swiftly as almost to elude the sight. Its wings, when it is balancing over the flower, produce a humming sound, which gives name to the bird. It is the smallest of the feathered race, and is one of the most beautiful in the elegance of its form, and the glossy brilliancy of its delicate plumage. Small as it is, however, it is exceedingly courageous, and has violent passions. If it find that a flower has been deprived of its honey, it will pluck it off, throw it on the ground, and sometimes tear it to pieces ; and it often fights with a desperate fury, which is astonishing in a creature of such diminutive size. It will even allow a man to come within two yards of it before it will take to flight. Humming birds are caught by blowing water on them from a tube, or shooting at them with sand,

The length of this bird is three inches ; it lives partly on honey obtained from flowers, but devours also great quantities of very small insects. The general color is a rich golden green on the upper parts. The breast and neck are of a dusky white.

The nest of this little bird is fixed on the upper side of the branch of a tree. Instances have been known of its building on an old moss-grown trunk, or on a strong weed in the garden ; but these cases are rare. The nest is about an inch in diameter and an inch deep, formed of gossamers, and of the downy substance from the great mullien. The female lays two eggs, which are of a pure white color. If any one approaches the nest, the little creatures dart around with a humming sound, frequently passing within a few inches of a person's head. His only note is a single chirp, not louder than that of a cricket or grasshopper.

The humming-bird is a general favorite. His flight from flower to flower resembles that of a bee, but is infinitely more rapid. He poises himself in the air, moving his wings so as to look like a thin and golden mist, while he thrusts his long slender bill into the flowers in search of food. He sometimes enters a room by the window, examines the flowers on the mantlepiece, and passes out by the opposite door or window.

THE LYRE-BIRD.

IF "all men are liars," there are also some lyre-birds. Here is one. He don't look as if he could be trusted, with all that burden of fuss and feathers on his back. It would seem as if any puff of wind would blow him over. "Right side up with care," would be a difficult matter in a gale. So it is with men-liars. Nothing keeps a man or a boy so straight, perpendicular, upright, as truthfulness. Nothing makes him top-heavy, unsteady, and unreliable, like a habit of lying.

THE MAY FLY.

"The Angler's May-fly is the most short-lived in its perfect state of any of the insect race, emerges from the water, where it passes its *aurelia* state about six in the evening, and dies about eleven at night."—*White's Selborne.*

The sun of the eve was warm and bright
  When the May-fly burst his shell,
And he wanton'd awhile in that fair light
  O'er the river's gentle swell;
And the deepening tints of the crimson sky
Still gleam'd on the wing of the glad May-fly.

The colors of sunset passed away,
  The crimson and yellow green,
And the evening-star's first twinkling ray
  In the waveless stream was seen;
Till the deep repose of the stillest night
Was hushing about his giddy flight

The noon of the night is nearly come—
  There's a crescent in the sky;—
The silence still hears the myriad hum
  Of the insect revelry.
The hum has ceas'd—the quiet wave
Is now the sportive May-fly's grave.

Oh! thine was a blessed lot—to spring
  In thy lustihood to air,
And to sail about, on untiring wing,
  Through a world most rich and fair,
To drop at once in thy watery-bed,
Like a leaf that the willow branch has shed.

And who shall say that his thread of years
  Is a life more blest than thine!
Has his feverish dream of doubts and fears
  Such joys as those which shine

In the constant pleasures of thy way,
Most happy child of the happy May!

For thou wert born when the earth was clad
  With her robe of buds and flowers,
And didst float about with a soul as glad
  As a bird in the sunny showers;
And the hour of thy death had a sweet repose,
Like a melody, sweetest at its close.

Nor too brief the date of thy cheerful race—
  'Tis its use that measures time—
And the mighty spirit that fills all space
  With His life and His will sublime,
May see that the May-fly and the Man
  Each flutter out the same small span.

And the fly that is born with the sinking sun
  To die ere the midnight hour,
May have deeper joy, ere his course be run,
  Than man in his pride and power;
And the insect's minutes be spared the fears
And the anxious doubts of our threescore years.

The years and the minutes are as one—
  The fly drops in his twilight mirth,
And the man, when his long day's work is done,
  Crawls to the self-same earth.
Great Father of each! may *our* mortal day
Be the prelude to an endless May.

THE CARRIER PIGEON.

THE CARRIER-PIGEON.

PIGEONS have been put to the remarkable purpose of acting as carriers of letters or other light objects. They have great power of flight, and will go long distances and never fail to return home. A particular species, larger than the common pigeon, is trained for the purpose, and in some countries the rearing of them forms a lucrative employment. The instinct which has rendered the carrier-pigeon so serviceable, is the strong desire manifested by all pigeons to return to the place of their residence; and man has adopted various measures to make their return on particular occasions more certain.

A male and female are usually kept together and treated well; and one of them, when taken elsewhere, is supposed to have the greater inducement to come back.

It is obvious that the carrier-pigeon can only be employed in conformity with some previously contemplated plan, for which the proper preparations have been made. It must have been taken from a place to which it is desired to return, and be temporarily at the place from which the intelligence is to be conveyed.

It is usually taken to that place hood-winked, or in a basket covered; the instinct by which it finds its way back, must therefore be independent of all knowledge of the intermediate places.

When the moment for employing it has arrived, the person requiring its services writes a message on a thin piece of paper, which is placed lengthwise under the wing, and fastened by a pin to one of the feathers. On being released, the carrier ascends to a great height, takes one or two turns in the air, and then commences its career at the rate of forty miles an hour, or about a thousand a day.

It was not long since a pigeon was employed in this way to carry messages between Hatifax and Boston. There are many pretty stories of the achievements of this bird in the affairs of love and romance, and it has often been the theme of poetry and of song.

BIRDS—"LITTLE BIRDS."

AS described by ornithologists, the instinct of certain kinds of birds—"little birds,"—leads them to lead an enemy away from their nests by pretending to be so wounded as to enable the pursuer to catch them easily. They will run along on the ground before the enemy, pretending to be unable to fly, but taking good care to keep out of real harm's way.

BIRDS SPEAKING ENGLISH.

A TRAVELER in South America, speaking of the birds of his native land, says it is pleasant to notice that, in whatever strange countries they may have wandered during winter, and whatever strange tongues they may have heard, they nevertheless come back *speaking English.* Hark! "Phœbe! Phœbe!" plain enough. And by-and-by the bobolink, saying, Bob o' Lincoln;" and the quail, saying, "Bob White." We have heard of one who always thought the robin said, "Skillet! skillet! three legs to a skillet! two legs to a skillet!" A certain facetious doctor says the robins cry out to him, as he passes along the road, "Kill 'em! cure 'em, physic! physic! physic!" The whip-poor-will talks English plain enough, the world over; but crows talk Dutch, and are the most accommodating birds in the world, for they always yield assent, with a "yaw, yaw, yaw," even if you ask leave to shoot them, but ten to one if they don't fly away while they say it.

Frogs, both great and small, talk excellent English. If you doubt, go and walk by the pond on a still May evening, and very likely they will tell you the the name of your sweetheart, or blaze to all the world something that you have been doing, and that you would rather not have made public.

CHRISTMAS WITH THE BIRDS.

EORGIE, what do you think becomes of all the little birds in the cold, northern countries, when the ground is covered with deep snow all the winter? It is a very hard time for them, I assure you, for there are only a few berries left on the trees; but some of them manage to live on these, and find a little corner in the thick straw roof of some friendly cottage. A great many feathered travelers fly away to warmer countries, where the winter is not so severe; but some that stay behind, perish with cold and hunger.

But I will tell you what the people in Norway do for them. They, as well as we, are very fond of having a "merry Christmas and a happy New-Year." Can you fancy a home among the mountains the day before Christmas? The snow is all over the house and garden, and all the country round; and though the sun shines on it, tinging it with beautiful colors, it does not melt it. Well, in-doors, every one is as busy as busy can be; even the children find something to do; for, most likely, a lot of little cousins are coming to spend Christmas with them. But not only do these kind people think of being happy and comfortable themselves,' but they do not forget the little birds out in the cold. So, before the sun sets, all the children are muffled up in furs and hoods, and go out to help in the fun of giving the birds a "Merry Christmas." The boys have great snow-shoes on, which are something like little boats, only narrower; and with these they slide about over the snow till they are quite warm. Presently the good man of the house comes out of the barn with a sheaf of unthreshed corn fastened on to a long pole; and a great shout the children set up as he comes. They then stick the pole into the ground by the side of the house, and the corn stands up, and looks as if it were inviting all the birds to come and have a feast. In a short time the birds come, twittering and chattering round the house, and flying into the sheaf, and getting out the full ripe corn; and more and more keep gathering round, till they make quite a large party.

When the sun sets, which it soon does, they go in and gather round a great fire made of pine-wood; and the boys bring in a large log to make a blaze; so the evening passes very merrily, as they sit round the fire, singing Christmas songs, or telling tales.

This custom of feeding the birds, is called "Juleskik,"* or "Christmas custom;" "*Jule*" meaning Christmas. Now, we are fond of having a good log on Christmas Eve, and you may have heard your elder brothers and sisters call it a "Yule Log."

* Pronounced Yuleskik.

Well, it is from this old Norwegian word that our word "Yule" is derived. Perhaps the Danes brought it with them when they came to England, for they speak the same language as the Norwegians.

Now, many children in England and America are fond of having Christmas parties. Would it not be nice if, at your next gathering, you could have this beautiful custom for a new game? You have Christmas trees, and those you have copied from the German children; could you not also take a lesson from the peasants in Norway? Many of you have the opportunity of gleaning a nice handful of corn from the harvest field; and besides this, crumbs of bread, biscuit, cheese, bread and milk, would be gladly accepted by these little denizens of the woods and lanes, who, in the bitter weather, approach the dwellings of man and ask his sympathy. There is your own pet robin, that will repay your kindness with his plaintive song, the next time the sun shines; the tiny wren, which hops about the cart-shed; and the blackbird that, for present kindness, will gladden you with his "mellow vesper-hymn" next April, as you walk by the wood-side. All these will teach you the true pleasure of doing good, and will be a great deal better than many games which only please yourselves.

we see around us have their regular hours for feeding, singing, bathing, resting, and sleeping.

We met a bird-hunter in Trinidad; he had been at work two years collecting near six hundred different kinds. He was of opinion there are over a thousand varieties of night and day birds to be found in the Madeira Plate, besides snakes, lizards, and any quantity of insects. Trinidad was his head-quarters from which he branched off in all directions during the dry season. His room was a perfect curiosity shop. The birds were rolled up in paper after they had been properly cured, and stowed away in large wooden boxes. Every day, at different hours, he went to the field; after days of labor, he would be seen returning with a single bird, differing from any in his room. He procures poisonous snakes by splitting the end of a stick to form a fork, which he places over the neck of the snake, and holds him until a gourd or bottle is fixed over his head, when he loosens his fork and the snake crawls into the cavity. He then corks the gourd and puts it into his pocket. After the snake starves to death, or is drowned in spirits, his skin is taken off, preserved, and stuffed, ready for transporting to the museums of the civilized world.

THE HERON.

WHO of you would imagine that there is any connection between the bird whose picture is given above, and the quaint old adage—

"He does not know a hawk from a handsaw."

And yet there is a connection between them, and that so intimate, that the *handsaw* of the proverb is nothing else than the heron itself. To explain this paradox, it is necessary only to recall to mind an old name of the heron, which was *heronshaw* or *hernshaw*. The proverb, "He does not know a hawk from a hernshaw," was expressive of stupidity—since these two birds were totally unlike, and could scarcely be confounded by any one possessed of common sense. The corruption of *hernshaw* into *handsaw*, has greatly marred the significance of the saying, which, however, is still in common use.

In ancient times the heronshaw was famous in the popular art of falconry. It was so much esteemed, both as an object of that aristocratic sport, and also as an article of food upon the tables of the great, that a fine of one pound was imposed upon any one who destroyed its eggs. In the times of Henry the Eighth, a heron was worth as much as a fine pheasant. But it was not only for sport or for food that this bird was esteemed.

The plumes which crown its head, and those which droop over the wings, were prized as ornaments; and their use was confined to the noble of the land.

The common heron (*cinerea ardea,*) is found extensively in various parts of the world. In England, it is quite common to find heronries like the rookeries, in the lofty trees which surround the fine old mansions of the country. Sometimes there is a feud between the herons and the rooks on account of the trees, and fierce battles have been known to take place between them. Generally, however, they peaceably divide the trees, and each party keeps to itself. The heron's nest is a rude structure of dry sticks, deposited in a crotch of the tree ; but it is carefully lined with wool, upon which are laid five blueish-green eggs. The uncouth appearance of the young herons may be conceived from the exceeding ugliness of the bird in full feather.

The heron is made by some naturalists a symbol of solitude, because it is accustomed to watch alone for its prey. It will stand perfectly motionless in a shallow pond or stream, and in the grey twilight of morning, may easily be mistaken for a stump. If closely watched, however, it will be seen suddenly to dart its strong sharp beak into the water, and almost unerringly strike and capture a fish for its breakfast, which it soars away to enjoy in its lofty nest.

The day of the heron seems to have gone by—not that the bird is becoming extinct or very scarce—but hawking is no longer a fashionable sport ; the flesh of the heron is no longer sought for by the gourmand, and the heron-plumes cannot now vie with ostrich feathers, or with cunning and delicate artificial fabrics, as ornaments for the head of beauty and pride.

FANNIE AND HER DEAD CHICKENS.

LITTLE Fannie had a brood of chickens that she attended with great care. At night she was particular to see that they were safely housed from all harm.

One evening she was busily engaged with an

interesting story, and when her mother asked her if it was not time to put up her chickens, she said,

"Oh, do wait a little longer, mother, I'm reading such a beautiful book. Wait just a minute."

This she repeated again and again, when her mother reminded her that it was getting late. At length she finished her story, and retired, forgetting her chickens. In the morning she arose, and on looking out of her window, she saw beneath her window, on large sticks, two dead chickens. She had given them the curious names of *Misses Indott* and *Individual.* And there was a placard, in large letters—

"Misses Indott and Individual departed this life early this morning. For the cause of their death, refer to Punctual Fannie."

This little girl, as you see from her appearance, is paying dear for her "Wait just a minute." And how many children bring upon themselves sorrow and trouble by this same habit of "waiting just a minute," instead of doing promptly what they are bidden. The untimely death of these poor chickens will teach a lesson to Fannie which she will not soon forget. And will not our young readers learn it, before they are taught it by their own sad experience.

THE UMBRELLA BIRD.

THIS singular bird is about the size of a raven, and is of a similar color, but its feathers have a more scaly appearance, from being margined with a different shade of glossy blue. It is also allied to the crow in its structure, being very similar to it in its feet and bill. On its head it bears a crest, different from that of any other bird. It is formed of feathers more than two inches long, very thickly set, and with hairy plumes curving over the end. These can be laid back so as to be hardly visible, or can be erected and spread out on every side, forming a hemispherical, or rather a hemiellipsoidal dome completely covering the head, and even reaching beyond the point of the beak; the individual feathers then stand out something like the down-bearing seeds of the dandelion. Besides this, there is another ornamental appendage on the breast, formed by a fleshy tubercle as thick as a quill, and an inch and a half long, which hangs down from the neck, and is thickly covered with glossy feathers, forming a long pendant plume or tassel. This also the bird can either press to its breast so as to be scarcely visible, or can swell out so as almost to conceal the fore part of its body. In the female the crest and the neck-plume are less developed, and she is altogether a smaller and much less handsome bird. It inhabits the wooded islands of the Rio Negro and the Solinoes, never appearing on the main land. It feeds on fruits and utters a loud, hoarse cry, like some deep musical instrument, whence its Indian name, *Uramimbe*, "trumpet-bird." The whole of the neck, where the plume of feathers springs from, is covered internally with a thick coat of hard, muscular fat very difficult to be cleaned away—which in preparing the skins, must be done, as it would putrefy, and cause the feathers to drop off.

THE NEST BUILDERS.

Oh! beautiful, beautiful things!
  How they range at will through the sky!
Dear Mary, if I could have wings,
  Oh! would'nt I, would'nt I fly?

I would float far away on the cloud,
  All veiled in the silver mist;
And perhaps I should feel so proud,
  I should'nt come back to be kissed.

But see, sis, the sweet little creatures
  Have each a straw in his beak;
A lesson of duty to teach us,
  As plainly as birds can speak.

We think they are only playing,
  As they roam to and fro in the sky;
But these busy fellows are saying,
  " 'Tis not all for pleasure we fly.

" We're building a snug little nest,
  In the crotch of the old elm-tree;
We mean it for one of the best,
  And busy enough are we.

" We would not live only for play,—
  And when for a song we take leisure,
We would show, in our caroling way,
  How duty is wedded to pleasure."

A SHORT CHAPTER ON BIRDS.

UITE probably you are all interested in birds. The Bible tells us that not even a little sparrow falls to the ground without our heavenly Father's notice. Do you suppose the cruel sportsmen think of this?

How beautiful and varied their plumage! What thrilling melody pours from their little throats, ascending like incense to their Creator! Now, instead of awakening us with their sweet notes, we see them winging their way southward. Often in the early dawn several small flocks pass. We call this wise preparation for the winter, instinct. It is God who maketh the stork to know times and seasons. Just this moment, a flock of twenty birds or so have alighted upon a cherry tree opposite my window. What a chattering! no soothing melodies as in spring, no snatches of song. They only utter short, twittering notes; often many endeavor to be heard at the same time. Now one flies to the topmost bough, then back again, uttering a sharp chirp; then all scold, then part consult in a moderate voice. It reminds me of one of the chats in the MUSEUM, for they are very earnest, and I fancy it is as important, for the birds are discussing winter arrangements. They have no wardrobes to prepare, like the city belles—who return to their homes. Now they are off, away over the wide plains, until they are lost to sight. They will return to their birth-place in the spring, and again enliven us with their glad rejoicings. I suppose that some of my readers do not know that the robin

THE SONGSTER.

at the South, during the winter, mopes away his time, seldom uttering more than a weak chirp. No little nest is made, no joyous outbursts of song as in New England. If you should chance to see him in the everglades of Florida or the wilds of Texas, you would hardly recognize red-breast. Bobolink, too, loses his mirthful voice, and is called a rail in Virginia, and a rice-bird in Carolina, where he fattens in the rice-fields in the last of autumn. I saw several in the West Indies. The natives call them brown birds—I never heard a song from one of them. So all lands have their peculiar charms, and the presence of singing birds adds greatly to our enjoyment in spring. Their migration affords us a lesson. We, too, are passing away, to the silent land of death! If we are prepared to go, we shall arise in the morning of the resurrection with songs of joy and everlasting gladness, praising our Savior who died to redeem us. Dear readers, have you accepted of His sacrifice? If not, no longer grieve Him by delay. Oh, give Him your hearts now, in the spring-time of existence! You may never see the *autumn* of life. Now only can you claim the promise · "They that seek me early, shall find me."

THE HOOPOE.

THIS bird seems to be top-heavy. At any rate, he has a very large top-knot, and one would think it would be hard work, with such a head, to fly against the wind.

The hoopoe is found in almost all parts of the old world, in Europe, Asia, and Africa. They have been seen as far north as Sweden, though they do not like cold countries. The Italians call it *bubola*. as that word very nearly represents its peculiar cry or note. It is a very shy bird at certain seasons, avoids being seen as much as possible, and hides itself in the thick wood. But it is not timid or modest about being heard. It keeps up a constant cry, *bu*, *bu*, *bu*, with a voice so clear and strange, that it can be heard at a great distance. It builds its nest and rears its young in the deep woods ; and it is during this period, that it seems so shy of being seen. Indeed, it is more afraid of exposing its young, than of incurring harm to itself. When the young ones are fledged, the birds may be seen in fine weather, in the fields and orchards in quest of food. Its nest is built in the hollow of an old tree, or in the deserted hole of a woodpecker. It is constructed chiefly of hair and feathers, and is very soft and nice.

THE HOOPOE.

THE WHIP-POOR-WILL.

THERE was once a boy, whose name I have forgotten; but, for the sake of having a name, we will call him Thomas. His father was a rich man, who had gained a great deal of money in New York, and so he bought a nice country residence in the northern part of New Jersey; and one summer day he removed thither with his wife and family.

Thomas, unfortunately, had acquired some bad habits in the city of New York. He did not like to study his lessons; and very often, when sent to school, he would roam about the streets, or go over to Hoboken; and having spent the day in this manner, he would go home and pretend he had been to school. He also made use of bad words, and told fibs, and disobeyed his parents.

It is quite surprising to see how one fault helps along others. A boy who is disobedient in one thing, will soon become so in many things: from disobedience he will pass to falsehood, from falsehood to unkindness, from unkindness to cruelty, and from all these to theft, and at last, perhaps, to robbery and murder. The path of evil is a down-hill path, and the further one goes in it, the nearer he is to the bottom, which is destruction.

Now Thomas, poor fellow, had gone a good way down the hill, and he found it so easy to go, that he did not care to stop. His parents were quite aware of his errors, and this was one reason why they bought a country house. They hoped, by taking their son from his evil companions and the many temptations in the great city, to cure him of his faults.

Thomas was delighted with the idea of going into the country to spend the summer. A thousand pleasant things rushed into his mind, as he thought of the hills and the villages, and the birds, and the squirrels, and fishes. He could scarce wait for the day of departure ; and when at last it did come, he bounded about as if his feet had springs in them. The journey occupied a whole day, and at night most of the family, being weary, retired early to rest.

Thomas was very unwilling to go to bed. It was a warm, moonlight night, and he desired to ramble about. His father and mother indulged him for a time, but when it came to be nine o'clock, they insisted on his going to his room. He pouted and fretted, but at last, with a very bad grace, he submitted.

Thomas' room was on the second floor, and the two windows looked out into the garden, which was very large and beautiful. The boy stood gazing from one of these windows for some time, when suddenly the idea came into his head that he might get out of the window, and by clinging to the branches of the trees, descend to the ground. He would then be free to walk about as long as he pleased.

This was no sooner thought than done, and in a few seconds Thomas found himself at liberty in the garden. Here he walked about for some time, and then passing out of the gate, he went into the lane that passed by the house. He continued to walk along for some time ; and though the place was rather lonesome, there being no house near, the youth found great pleasure in the novelty of the scene. He continued to walk on for an hour, and then he turned back, intending to go home. He, however, took a wrong path, and this soon led him into the wood. He became aware that he had lost his way, yet he only walked on the faster. His heart began to beat, and a kind of cold, creeping sensation came over his skin. There was a bristling sort of feeling in his head, and his cap rose up at least an inch.

Thomas would have been very glad to be at home, and his anxiety did not diminish when he found that the scene around became more dark and wild, while at the same time his knees knocked against each other, and his under jaw made a strange clattering against the upper one. But what could he do? He paused a moment to consider : at the same time a kind of faintness came over him, and he was obliged to sit down.

In a few moments this feeling passed away, but the youth was by no means at ease. He was conscious of having gone out by stealth ; and, as usual in such cases, the sense of this one fault brought on him the recollection of others. "After all," said conscience to him, "you are a very bad boy, Thomas; you are disobedient; you deceive your parents; you care not for them or their commands; you love only yourself. You are in a very bad way—what will become of you?"

Scarcely had this train of thought crossed his bosom, when a soft, distant voice was heard in the woods, crying: "WHIP HIM WELL!—WHIP HIM WELL! WHIP HIM WELL!"

Thomas' blood grew cold, and his hair bristled, and his teeth chattered. All was silent for a few moments. He sat listening intently, yet fearing to hear the dreadful cry repeated. It soon began; and now it was nearer, and louder, and clearer:—

"*Whip him well! Whip him well! Whip him well!*"

Again all was silent. It is impossible to express the emotions of remorse, terror and amazement which filled the bosom of our hero at this moment. It was near midnight; he was lost; he was also in an unknown wilderness; the moon had gone down; the darkness and gloom gave to the trees around the grisly aspects of giants and monsters; all was still as in the valley of the shadow of death, save only that wild, elvish cry, "Whip him well! Whip him well!"

As it burst out a third time, it seemed close at his side, and rang louder than ever in his ear. He could bear it no longer. Uttering a yell of horror, he sprang to his feet and fled. For some time he flew along the path that wound through the woods, almost as if he had wings. Being at last very weary, he began to slacken his pace, when he heard the terrible admonition—

"Whip him well!—Whip him well!" bursting from twenty voices out of the trees around. Fear lent him wings; and on he went, not thinking or knowing whither. Yet, strange to say, the terrible voices pursued him. At last, he came to the edge of the woods, and suddenly he was among open grounds and cultivated fields. The dawn of the morning had begun, and looking round, the boy saw a farm at a distance; as he drew near, he discovered it to be his home.

Never was joy greater than his. He went into the garden, climbed the trees, and entered his chamber. But it was a long time before he left it. The next morning, his parents found him suffering from fever. They discovered that his feet, and face, and hands, were scratched in a strange manner; and at last he told his mother of his terrible adventures. After hearing his story, she spoke to him as follows:

"My dear Thomas, let this incident be made useful to you. What you have seen and heard is easily explained. The awful cry in the woods was only the song of the Whip-poor-will. It is an innocent bird, hiding itself by day; but at night it fills the woods with its shrill, wild notes. It was your disturbed conscience, Thomas, that made it terrible, and so it is always. A mind at ease, a heart assured of Heaven's favor, is tranquil and happy, while the bosom of the wicked is the seat of terror and dismay. The slightest trouble, the commonest dangers, to bad men, are rendered heavy calamities by their bad consciences. Their bosoms are full of fear and dread. At night, they start and shiver in the dark ; every sound disturbs them : to their uneasy mind, a bush is a ghost, and a rock a monster. The trees seem like giants, and their spreading branches like hooked claws or fingers. The dreams of the wicked are full of dreadful scenes, horrid noises, and terrible adventures.

"Such, my dear Thomas, are the effects of misconduct, which begets a bad conscience. It is the dispensation of Providence that sin leaves its impressions on the soul, and the soul must suffer for it. There is no escape but by genuine repentance, and the washing out of the stain by God's forgiveness."

Many other things of this kind did the good mother say to her son, and when, after a few weeks, he rose from his bed, he was a better and a happier child. But, during his whole life, he could not bear the lone, wild, hurried cadences of the Whip-poor-will, without a cold, creeping sensation over his skin—a sort of upraising of his hair.

NEST OF THE TITMOUSE.

BIRDS are very skilful architects, so far as constructing their own houses are concerned, yet their skill is merely instinctive, no progression or improvement ever being made. The first essay of the young bird is as perfect as the nest of a veteran songster. There is a great difference in the abilities of birds each building according to its circumstances and wants, from a simple indentation in the naked sand up to the swinging castle in the air constructed of down and hair.

Among the nests of remarkable construction may be reckoned that of the Long Tailed Titmouse, illustrated above. This bird, which is not bigger than a wren, and is almost incessantly in motion, takes innumerable means of precaution for the comfort, safety and concealment of its dwelling. It is made like a hollow ball, with a small opening on one side, as may be seen in the engraving. This orifice serves the double purpose of door and window, and is so well barricaded that neither cold nor rain can penetrate into the interior. This is effected by an admirably contrived screen, before the entrance to the little citadel, of downy feathers, which is very pliant, to admit of ingress and egress, and yet exclude the weather. Yet this is not all. From its very diminutive size, this bird is afraid of numerous enemies, and, therefore, has recourse to wise artifice to con-

THE SWALLOW-TAILED KITE

IS an inhabitant of North America. It feeds on the wing, like the swallow, pursuing the large moths and other insects, with ease and rapidity. These insects are not their only food, Audubon says they eat large grasshoppers, caterpillars. small snakes, lizards, and f.ogs. They fly close over the fields, secure a snake, and holding it fast by the neck, carry it off, and devour it in the air. Its nest is upon the top of an old pine, or oak—eggs from four to six ; of a greenish white, and spotted with brown at the large end. Length of the bird is two feet.

THE TOUCAN.

THIS bird is one of the most extraordinary in the world. It is remarkable for a monstrous bill, which is from six to seven inches in length, and in some places two in breadth, the whole being extremely slight, and a little thicker than parchment. The plumage of this bird is dark, spotted with blue, purple, yellow and other colors that produce a very beautiful effect. The legs, feet, and claws are of an ash color; and the toes stand like those of parrots, two before, and two behind. The tongue is feathered at the edges, and, as well as the inside of the mouth, is of a deep red.

The toucan is easily tamed, and will become very familiar, eating almost any thing offered to it. In general, it feeds upon fruits. In its wild state it is a noisy bird, perpetually moving from place to place in search of food. It is particularly fond of grapes. If these were plucked from the stalk one by one, and thrown to it, the toucan will catch them with great dexterity before they fall to the ground.

When in flocks, these birds generally appoint one of their number to watch through the night. While they are asleep, he sits perched at the top of a tree above them, making a continual noise, resembling ill-articulated sounds, and moving his head during the whole time to the right and left. From this circumstance, the South Americans have given this bird the name of the preacher.

SEVEN BIRDS' NESTS.

AS I was traveling in the country, the other day, I counted, on some bushes in the highway, almost within a stone's throw of a dwelling house in which was a large family of little children, no less than seven birds' nests.

Now you cannot find seven birds' nests in the highway, near our cities and large towns, in walk ing a mile. Indeed you will rarely find *one*. But why not, as well as in the country? I will tell you.

In cities and towns there are a great many idle, lazy, men and boys, who have nothing better to do —that is, they will do nothing better—than to take their fowling pieces, and go and shoot birds. Some they kill; some they wound; others they frighten. This is one reason why birds and birds' nests are not more numerous in such places.

Another thing is that the city and town boys are very apt to rob the nests, either of their eggs or their young. Birds do not like, better than men, to see their houses pillaged and destroyed, and their little ones cruelly treated and enslaved; so they flee to other places or countries. And I would, if I were they.

Where there has been, for fifty or a hundred years, no cruel hunting, trapping, ensnaring, or robbing of birds, it is surprising to see how tame many sorts of them are. They will come and sit on the lilac, or rose, or quince bushes, close by the window; and if they do not actually build nests and rear young there—for the ugly cat will sometimes prevent this—they will sing to Robert and John, and to the rest of the inmates of the family, many a sweet morning song.

THE PEACOCKS.

HERE was a gentleman who had two peacocks which were kept in a fine lawn in his garden; and he made a present of them to his daughter, Miss Charlotte Fletcher, who was very fond of them, and fed them herself every day. One of these peacocks was very beautiful; he had a fine long tail, which trailed after him as he walked, and which he frequently spread out for the admiration of those who stopped to look at him. But this peacock was not so good as he was handsome; for he was proud, greedy, and ill-natured; and because the other peacock, which was a *white one*, had not so fine a plumage as himself, he despised him, and very often was so cross, that he would scarcely let the poor bird have any thing to eat, but pecked him, and drove him about in a cruel manner; and if at any time the white peacock spread out his tail, the other would, set up such a frightful scream, as made him close it up directly, and run away into some corner to hide himself.

When these birds were given to Miss Fletcher,

she admired that with the fine plumage, and said he should be called her *handsome favorite*, for she did not know of his faults ; neither did he treat the other ill in her sight for some time ; but, one day, when she was feeding them from the parlor window, she happened to throw some barley to the white peacock first, on which the other put himself in a violent passion, and set up one of his horrid screams, which she was quite shocked to hear ; nor was this all, for the cross creature flew upon the other peacock, and tore him about till he pulled off a great many feathers, and made his head bleed sadly ; and the white peacock could not defend himself, because he had the misfortune to have his leg broken soon after he left the nest, and was, in consequence of the accident, a little lame. However, he contrived to get away to his hiding place, while the other greedy creature was picking up the barley ; and, when his meal was ended, the ill-natured peacock strutted about as proud and conceited as could be, before the window, and spread out his fine tail, expecting to be admired as usual. But Miss Fletcher was too good to like the bird which was so cross to his companion ; on the contrary, she was quite displeased with him, and sent the gardener to take him off the lawn, and carry him into the yard, where the common poultry was kept, and where he would be sure of getting well beat and pecked himself if he showed any airs ; and she said, he should be no longer her ***handsome favorite***, but she would take care of the white peacock, and try to get him a better companion ; so she desired Thomas to find out where he was hidden, and to bring him to her. It was quite grievous to see how sadly the poor creature was hurt ; but he was very patient, and, in a short time, by being well

fed and kept quiet, he recovered and was sent back to the lawn again.

In the mean time the proud peacock was greatly mortified at being kept in a common farm-yard, where nobody troubled themselves about him, and where the cock and hens made him keep his distance while they were feeding, and content himself with what he could pick up when they had done. He now wished he had not treated his former companion so ill; and sometimes he would get up upon the barn and call out, in hopes that the other peacock would hear him, and know how sorry he was, and that he was resolved never to behave so ill again; which made the white peacock desirous of having him back, and he let him know this by answering to him from the top of a pear-tree in the garden. Miss Fletcher hearing the two birds call to one another in this manner, and observing that the white peacock seemed very dull, thought that perhaps they might have made up their quarrel, so she resolved to see how they would behave to one another; and, to her very great delight, when the servant, by her desire, brought the cross peacock from the place of punishment, the other ran to meet him on the lawn, and was very glad to see him; and when she threw some barley to them, the peacock which before had been so greedy, did not peck a grain from the other; nor did he ever after treat him ill in any way, but became as *good* as he was *pretty*. Miss Fletcher, however, did not call him her *handsome favorite*, but gave the preference to the white peacock, because the other had not been *always* good and she resolved for the future to value things, not from their showy qualities, but from their real and intrinsic worth. Beauty and fine clothing may attract notice, but kindness and generosity win true friends.

THE BLACKBIRD.

THE little story I have to tell you is about a blackbird. You all know that the blackbird sings a very fine song; and how delightful it is to hear him, on a fine summer morning or evening, pouring forth his rich notes, causing the woods to ring with the melody of his lovely voice. The blackbird I have to tell you about built its nest in a large bush in the corner of a garden belonging to a working man. This good man paid a goodly rent for his garden. But his little boys and girls, as they grew up, assisted him to keep and dress it. The apples and pears, and all the nice things that grew in the garden, were sold to buy food and clothing for his wife and family.

I think I hear you saying, that is all very good; but what about the blackbird;

Well, I will tell you presently. The blackbird built its nest in one of the largest bushes in the garden. These kind people did not pull down the nest, nor cruelly destroy the young ones, but rather protected and assisted the mother to rear her little family, by laying down food in sight of the nest. This little act of kindness so gained the love and confidence of the blackbird, that she grew so familiar with them that she would allow them to stand and look at her without stirring from the nest.

As they increased their attention and kindness, so did her confidence increase also; for, by and by, she would lift up, first the one wing, and then the other wing, and allow her kind protectors to have a peep at her interesting family; while the father, at no great distance, sat perched upon the uppermost bough of a tree, singing in his best style, pluming himself in all the pride of a delighted parent, to see his companion and offspring so much taken notice of and cared for.

Now, my dear young friends, you may see, from this little story, how much pure pleasure may be got from the exercise of a little kindness. These kind people did not only enjoy a large amount of real pleasure, arising out of an act of kindness to these defenceless creatures, but also a pretty large amount of profit. As soon as the story of the blackbird became known, numbers of people went to the garden, to see this natural curiosity, and make their purchases. Some would buy one thing, some another. In this way the gardener, with his family, was amply rewarded for their attention and kindness to these lovely songsters of the wood.

My dear young friends, we may also learn, from this little story, how amply our heavenly Father would reward us, if we would only be kind to each other, and to the inferior creatures he has made.

Before taking leave of my youthful readers, I would say, Do not rob a poor bird of her young. It is an act of very great cruelty. Do not torment nor beat any dumb creature whatever. Be kind to them all, and you will be surprised and delighted with the affection and gratitude you will receive in return.

THE DODO.

THIS bird, instead of being designed for swiftness, looks as if it was among the most stupid of living things. It was a native of the Isle of France, and was common there many years ago, but it is now extinct. It was an enormous creature, and would have made a meal for twenty or thirty men.

The dodo was originally found on the uninhabited islands in the Indian ocean, and in great numbers; but from various accounts, it is supposed now to have entirely disappeared.

The dodo, or as it is sometimes called, the solitary bird, or solitaire, was seen in large numbers on the islands of Bourbon and Mauritius, by the Portugese navigators, three centuries ago. They were then described as very tame, and not afraid of men.

Though they are clumsy to look at, they are described as graceful in their movements, and dignified in their bearing, and even beautiful.

They would allow themselves to be caught, but were incapable of being tamed, and would refuse all nourishment. Their nest was made of a heap of palm leaves, raised a foot and a half from the ground, into which one egg was deposited.

When the dodo finally disappeared from the islands is not known, but no traces of it have been found since the commencement of the eighteenth century.

THE EGYPTIAN VULTURE.

THIS bird, from its abundance in Egypt, is called "Pharoah's chicken." It is about the size of a raven. The chest and throat are naked; the general plumage of the male bird is white, with the quills black. This species ranges pretty extensively over the eastern continent. It follows the caravans in the deserts in large flocks, in order to feed upon the camels and other animals which perish in these hazardous marches, which are fatal to the lives of so many ; not only from the heat and drought, but from the piercing cold of the night, which often follows a burning hot day.

The ancient Egyptians paid divine honors to these birds, and we often find them represented in their sculptures and paintings ; and though the Mussulmans of the present day do not actually worship them, they treat them with much respect, as very important birds, in a country where cleanliness is so essential but so much neglected. They act as scavengers, picking up and devouring all sorts of animal and vegetable refuse. When pressed by hunger, they will gorge the most offensive substances.

They have a long, slender beak ; the nostrils are oval, and the head and neck bare of feathers, thus enabling them to burrow in the putrid carcass upon which they prey, without the risk of soiling their plumage. It is a curious fact that the claws of the vultures are so formed that they cannot clasp their prey with sufficient force to carry it away, and are therefore obliged to eat it on the spot.

THE LOVES OF BIRDS.

POETS have sung the loves of men and angels, but they have never been known to sing of the loves of birds. They have been very neglectful in this respect. The loves of birds would form as fruitful a theme as those of the poets themselves. In their attachments they are generally faithful and affectionate—and it must be confessed they are, like men, a little jealous sometimes. Audubon gives a beautiful description of the loves of humming-birds. He says that in their courtship, the male, dancing airily upon the wing, swells his plumage and throat, and whirls lightly around the female; and then diving towards a flower, he returns with loaded bill, which he proffers to her. He seems full of ecstacy when his caresses are kindly received. His little wings fan her as they fan the flowers, and he transfers to her bill the insect and the honey which he has procured. If his addresses are received with favor, his courage and care are redoubled. He dares even to chase the tyrant fly-catcher, and hurries the blue bird and martin to their nests; and then, on sounding pinions, he joyously returns to his lovely mate. Who would not be a humming-bird? Audubon says:

"Could you, kind readers, cast a momentary glance at the nest of the humming-bird, and see, as I have seen, the newly hatched pair of young, little larger than the bumble-bees, naked, blind, and so feeble as scarcely to be able to raise their little bills to receive food from their parents, full of anxiety and fear, passing and repassing within a few inches of your face, alighting on a twig not more than a yard from your body, awaiting the result of your unwelcome visit in a state of the utmost despair—you could not fail to be impressed with the deepest pangs which parental affection feels on the unexpected death of a cherished child. Then how pleasing is it, on your leaving the spot, to see the returning hope of the parents, when, after examining the nest, they find their nurslings untouched!"

We have remarked above that birds, as well as men, are sometimes jealous in love. An exception, however, may be found to this general rule in the golden-winged woodpecker, a frequent and well-known inhabitant of our American forests. Among the bright beaux and belles of this interesting tribe no jealousies seem to exist, and no quarrels ever occur. Cheerily they hop through life, attended by the good wishes of all their acquaintances, and of each other. No sooner does spring call them to the pleasant duty of selecting mates and pairing off, than their voices may be heard from the tops of high, decayed trees, proclaiming with delight the opening of the welcome season. Their note at this period is merriment itself, and when heard at a little distance resembles a prolonged and jovial laugh. These golden-winged woodpeckers are the darlings of Audubon. In describing their manner of mating, he says that several males surround a female, and to prove the truth and earnestness of their love, bow their heads, spread their tails, and move sideways, backwards and forwards, performing such antics as would induce any one witnessing them to join his laugh to theirs. The female joyfully flies to another tree, where she is closely followed by her suitors, and where again the same ceremonies are gone through with until a marked preference is indicated for some individual.

In this way, all the golden-winged woodpeckers are soon happily mated, and each pair proceeds to excavate a hole in a tree for a nest. They work alternately, with industry and apparent pleasure. When the nest is finished they caress each other on the tree top, rattle their bills against the dead branches, chase their cousins the red head, defy the purple grakles to enter their nest, and feed plentifully on ants, beetles, and larvæ. By and by the female lays four or six eggs, the whiteness and transparency of which are doubtless the delight of her heart. These woodpeckers raise a numerous progeny, having two broods every season.

The loves of the turtle-dove and mocking-bird are graphically described by Audubon, as are also those of the wild turkey, who is said to be even more ridiculous in his motions, and more absurd in his demonstrations of affection, than is our common tame gander. The curious evolutions in the air of the great horned owl, or his motions when he has

THE GOLDEN EAGLE.

THIS is one of the largest and noblest of all those birds that have received the name of eagle. The length of the female is three feet and a half; it weighs from sixteen to eighteen pounds; but the male seldom weighs above twelve pounds. Its bill is three inches long, and of a deep blue; and the eye of a very brilliant hazel color. The sight and sense of smelling are very acute. The head and neck are clothed with narrow sharp pointed feathers, of a deep brown color, bordered with tawny ones; but those on the crown of the head, in very old birds, turn gray.

There are numerous species of eagles, all of which are generally found in mountainous and ill-peopled countries, and breed among the loftiest cliffs. They choose those places most remote from man for their residence, and build their nests on the inaccessible cliffs. These are sometimes protected by a jutting crag but are frequently wholly exposed to the winds; for they are flat, though built with great labor. It is said that the same nest serves the eagle during life, and the pains bestowed in forming it would seem to authorize that belief. When a male and female have paired they remain together till death.

The eagle is at all times a formidable neighbor. He carries away hares, lambs, and kids; often destroys fawns and calves, to drink their blood, and carries a part of their flesh to his retreat. An instance is related in Scotland of two children being carried off by eagles: they fortunately received no harm by the way, and were restored unhurt out of the nests to the affrighted parents.

EAGLE FEEDING HER YOUNG.

Some time ago, it happened that a peasant resolved to rob the nest of an eagle, that had built in a small island in the beautiful lake of Killarney. He accordingly stripped and swam in upon the island, while the old ones were away; and robbing the nest of its young, he was preparing to swim back, with the eaglets tied in a string. While he was yet up to his chin in the water, the old eagles returned, and missing their young quickly fell upon the plunderer, and despite of all his resistance, dispatched him with their beaks and talons.

Of all animals the eagle flies highest, and on this account he was called by the ancients the Bird of Jove. Of all birds, too, he has the quickest eye, but his sense of smelling is far inferior to that of the vulture. His principal aliment is raw flesh.

The plumage of the eaglets is not so strongly marked as it is when they come to be adult. They are at first white, then inclined to yellow, and at last light brown. Age, hunger, long captivity, and diseases, make them whiter. It is said that they live above an hundred years ; and that they at last die, not of old age, but from the beak turning inwards upon the mandible, and thus preventing their taking any food. They are indeed equally remarkable for their longevity and for their power of sustaining a long abstinence from food.

The descriptions of the Golden Eagle given by systematic authors correspond but little with the name. Willoughby says, that, " the small feathers of the whole body are a dark ferruginous or chestnut ;" Linnæus, that " the body is variegated with brown and rusty ;" Latham, that the " head and neck are deep brown, the feathers bordered with tawny, hind-head bright rust color, body dark brown ;" Bewick, that " the general color is deep brown, mixed with tawny on the head and neck ;" Fleming, that " the acuminated feathers on the head and neck are bright rust color, the rest of the plumage dusky brown;" Baron Cuvier, that it is "more or less brown;" Temminck, that "the young at the age of one or two years have all the plumage of a ferruginous or reddish brown, clear and uniforn on all parts of the body;" and in proportion as they advance in age the colors of the plumage "at first is white, then faint yellow, and afterwards it becomes a bright copper color."

Belon even ventures to infer that when Aristotle first used the term golden, he did not mean that it was gilded, but only rather more reddish than other species. But on turning to the passage in Aristotle, we find that he says expressly, that, "the color is yellow."

THE WASHINGTON EAGLE.

THE LITTLE CHILD AND THE ROBINS.

To an elm tree close by our window,
  Two dear little robins have come,
And up in its shady green branches,
  Have made them a beautiful home.

The green leaves soft waving above them
  And the roof that o'ershadows their nest,
And the wind whispering gently around them,
  Is the music that lulls them to rest.

When the sun comes up from the shadows,
  To tell that a new day is born,
They wake up, these two little robins
  And hail the bright light with a song.

And soon their sweet carols of gladness
  Awaken me out of my dreams,
And I find that the glorious sun shine
  Is flooding the room with its beams.

And I offer my prayer of thanksgiving,
  To the great God who dwells up on high,
Who takes care of the birds and the children,
  And not one forgotten shall die.

And every night before sleeping,
  When the light I no longer can see,
I pray to my Father in Heaven,
  To take care of the birdies and me.

And I know if I'am good and obey him,
  I'll be happy all my life long,
Till at length, in that beautiful Heaven
  I shall praise him forever in song.

THE WILD TURKEY.

THIS beautiful bird is abundant in the wooded and uncultivated parts of the Western States, and the vast forests of the great valley of the Mississippi.

In the fall of the year, it spreads itself through the country in search of food, upon which its migrations depend. (This period is called by the Indians the *turkey months.*) These are made entirely on foot, till the turkeys reach the river. They then ascend to the tops of tall trees, and, at the cluck of their leader, fly to the opposite bank, the young ones sometimes falling into the water and drowning. Their speed is very considerable, and, when molested, they run with the velocity of a hound. After long journeys in frosty weather, they sometimes associate with the poultry near farm-houses, and enter the barns for grain. During this season great numbers are killed by the inhabitants, who preserve them in a frozen state and transport them to a distant market.

The female lays her eggs in April, in a hole slightly scratched in the ground, and covered with withered leaves. These she studiously conceals, and seldom abandons, and hatches from ten to fifteen young birds. The care and tenderness of the parent is now evinced by watching for the slightest danger, and resorting to places where there is the best supply of fruit and berries.

THE HAWKING PARTY.

FALCONRY was the favorite field-sport of the middle ages; but since the invention of guns with firelocks, it seems to have declined, as guns are a much more effectual means of bringing down game than the use of falcons and hawks.

Some of our young readers may ask what falconry is; we reply that it is a process of taking feathered game by the use of falcons, hawks, eagles or other rapacious birds, that are trained to the business, just as dogs are trained to pursue the hare, the fox, or the deer. Sometimes the sport was called hawking, as the falcon is a species of hawk. Falconry, while it existed, was the peculiar sport of kings and nobles, many of whom are now represented in their portraits with their favorite hawk seated on their wrist, thus showing the special regard in which they held the animal that gave them so much amusement.

The training of falcons to pursue their game and return again to their owners was a laborious and difficult process. It was necessary to take them when they were very young, and by slow steps teach them what was to be done. When the falcon did as was required, it was fed, and thus made to know that it had done right. If it was refractory and disobeyed, a cold stream of water was poured on its head, as an admonition that it had done wrong.

It was said to be a gallant and goodly sight when a large train of well-mounted English ladies and gentleman rode forth on a clear day to pursue this sport, attended by falconers, each with his hawk on his wrist.

Dogs were used to start the game, and then at a proper time the hawk was let loose to pursue it as it soared upward in the air. The ærial conflict often became intensely exciting to the lookers on. If one hawk was not sufficient to bring down the game, another and another were let loose, till victory was achieved, and the conqueror and the conquered came down rapidly to the ground, amid the shouts of the gay party.

THE PARTRIDGE.

THE partridge, properly speaking, is not a native of the United States. The bird called partridge in New England, is actually a species of grouse. The bird called quail in that part of the Union, and partridge at the south, is both unlike the true quail and partridge of Europe, though it resembles both. There is a very beautiful bird called a quail in California, about the size of our common species; and in South America there are other varieties; but it does not appear that the true partridge is found on our continent. This is one of those curious instances, among thousands of others, in which the natural products of the New World resemble those of the Old, yet never, or very rarely, becoming identical. It is strange that among all our thrushes, jays, sparrows, linnets, pigeons, and doves—among all our deer. squirrels, wolves, foxes, and hares—nay, even among all oaks, elms, walnuts, and maples—we have not a single species which finds it exact representative in Europe, Asia, or Africa.

The quails and partridges are regarded as one genus, and, taken together, they are a most interesting family. Probably there are at least a hundred species, and though some are large, and some are small—though some whistle and some only peep—though some live in the polar regions of the north, and others in the hot climate near the equator—they are everywhere the same gentle race, seeking cultivated fields, and dwelling in the vicinity of man, even though he is their greatest enemy. They lay a large number of eggs, and hatch broods of ten to eighteen at a time. The female is most devoted to her young ones, and often employs many stratagems to lead a pursuer away, so that her offspring may escape. Her young chickens have a wonderful instinct in eluding danger, and will often baffle the keenest eye, by hiding under leaves, or crouching under sticks and stones, until it is safe to leave their concealment

THE OSTRICH RIDER.

LET the fur-clad Laplander boast
  Of the reindeer's bird-like speed—
Let the Arab, for riding post,
  Bet high on his mettlesome steed;—

Let the Briton talk loud of the chase
  With the Fox, or the hare, or the stag;
Let the Yankee, stark mad in the race,
  Count miles by the minutes, and brag;-

The bird of the desert is ours—
  Competitors all we defy—
A bird of such wonderful powers,
  We scarce know if we ride or we fly.

You have all of the hippogriff heard,
For metal and speed a rare thing,
Half-breed betwixt courser and bird,
Keeping pace with foot and with wing.

The bird of the desert is he,
The ostrich of beautiful plume,
Skimming earth, as a swallow the sea,
Or an eagle the lofty blue dome.

He laughs at the speed of the hind,
For pursuers he feels no concern,
He travels ahead of the wind,
And leaves the dull lightning astern.

THE OSTRICH.

A TRAVELER in Africa says, no captive ostrich exhibited in zoological garden or menagerie can give any just idea of the native bird. Reaching at times the height of eight or nine feet, it weighs from 200 to 300 pounds, and has strength enough to kill, with a blow of his foot, a panther, a jackal, or a hyena. The most incredible stories are told of its speed of foot. One traveler asserts that an ostrich, with two men on its back, outstripped a fleet horse. It leaps over the plain in bounds of from twelve to fourteen feet, its claws hardly seeming to touch the ground. From man it invariably tries to escape, but its devices are not so stupid as some books on natural history would lead us to suppose. When a pair of ostriches with their young are attacked, the male ostrich will separate himself from his family and at a short distance pretend to be wounded and roll on the ground. The hunter runs towards him to secure him, but the cunning bird is up and off again in proper time—meanwhile the mother with her young have had a good start. The ostrich is graminivorous when there is any vendure to be had—otherwise he will eat sticks and stones. The egg of an ostrich is said to be equal to twenty-four hen's eggs, and the flavor is very superior.

Ostriches are very often killed by stratagem. A native covers a saddle or cushion with ostrich feathers, and shoulders it. His legs he whitens, and in his hands he holds a head and neck of an ostrich, through which a pliant stick has been thrust. Thus disguised, he trots out into the plain, picking up the grass with his sham head, and shaking his feathers, after the most approved ostrich fashion. His new fellow-creatures stare, but after a while set him down for a real ostrich, and continue their repast or gambols. Suddenly one of them tumbles down, struck by a poisoned arrow. The whole flock gallop off in a fright; but the most astonished of the party is the new-comer, who runs at double quick speed, and takes care to sidle up to the strongest males for protection. In this way, a man has been known to slay eight or ten fine birds in a day. It is a trick almost equal to that of some of the honest politicians of our day, who put on the cloak of friendship for some great measure, only to secure a favorable opportunity to smother it at last.

THE BIRD'S NEST.

WHO taught the pretty little bird
  To build her nest so well,
In which herself and family
  Might find a place to dwell?

She gathered grass from the green field,
  And hair, and straw, and hay,
And wandering string, and vagrant hair
  And spent thus many a day.

With her small beak und tiny claws
  She wove all these together,
And built herself a nice round nest,
  To keep out wind and weather.

And soon there were three pretty eggs,
  As blue as they could be,
And by-and-by you might have seen,
  Wee birdies—one, two, three!

What were the names of these young birds?
  Why, "Tom," and "Dick," and "Sallie;"
Ere many days they all could fly
  Far over hill and valley.

'Tis God that taught the parent bird
  To build so nice a dwelling,
To weave her wondrous little nest,
  In beauty rare excelling.

And if God cares for little birds,
  Much more for us he'll care,
And every thing that we shall want,
  He will for us prepare.

FREDERICK had found a bird's nest in the garden. It was almost concealed among the flowers and leaves of a tall rose bush. He had cautiously crept near it, and how happy he was to find that it contained young ones.

He carefully took the nest from the branch where it was placed, and showed it to his little brother and sister.

"O, brother," said little Agnes, "one of the birds

must be mine, and must be named Pecksy, like the little robin in the story book."

"And one must be mine," said little Robert, "and I shall want to tie a string to him, and hold him so he can never, never fly away."

"We must get a strong cage for them in the first place," said Frederic, "and take care of them, and let them grow up into big birds, for now the poor little things cannot fly, or do any thing for themselves.'

"Who takes care of the little birds when they are so young?" said Agnes.

"O, their father and mother birds, to be sure; they find worms and bugs, and carry them in their little bills, and drop them into the mouths of the young ones, and that I suppose is the reason that these little fellows have their mouths so wide open; they are expecting the old birds to bring them something."

Just then the children perceived two robins fluttering about them, making a very piteous noise, and the little birds in the nest opened their mouths wider, and peeped as loud as they could.

"I dare say," said Frederic, "that is the father and mother of our little birds, and I am thinking that they know a great deal better than we do, how to take care of their young ones, and I think I had better put the nest back where I found it."

"I think so, too," said little Agnes, "for perhaps the little birds would not have a very good time in the cage; and besides, we have not got any cage, and I am not quite sure that mother would like to have us take away the birds from their father and mother."

Little James, who did not understand the matter very well, still persisted that he wanted his bird, that he might tie a string to it, and then if it flew up in the air, he could get it again when he pleased.

But Frederic told him the bird would be unhappy to be so treated, and that he would ask cousin Maria to cut him a bunch of paper birds, which would spread out their wings, and who would not feel pain, if he pulled the string ever so hard.

This satisfied little James, and Frederic then placed the nest exactly where he had found it, in the rose bush, and the children all went to a little distance and kept quite still.

In a moment the old birds came back to the nest, and such a chirping and fluttering as took place never was seen. The little ones were probably telling how dreadfully they had been frightened, and old Mr. and Mrs. Robin were so happy, and they praised little Frederic so much, and declared whenever they saw him come into the garden, they would sing one of their very best songs.

Frederic's mother told him he had done quite right in putting the nest back. He had better, another time, not take a nest down at all, as sometimes the old birds were so frightened when they found the nest moved, that they flew away, and did not come back again. Cousin Maria cut James the paper birds, which pleased him so much, that he thought no more of the nest ; and the young robins grew up into very fine birds, and ate up so many canker worms and caterpillars, that Frederic's father's garden was the wonder of the neighborhood.

THE GARDEN.

WILD PIGEONS IN PARIS.

THERE is no bird more timid and wild than the pigeon in its natural state ; yet, by gentle treatment and breeding about the house, it becomes very tame. It is true that there are several kinds of pigeons, and some are more easily tamed than others.

The common house pigeon is a peculiar species, and more readily becomes domesticated than others. Perhaps our long-tailed, swift pigeon, called the *passenger*, could hardly be made to live about the house at all. Even if one of them were hatched in a pigeon house, we suspect that when his wings and tail were full grown, he would fly away over the hills and valleys, and never come back again to thank any body for his bringing up.

In France there is a fine, large species, called the *wild pigeon.* It is of a bluish color, its neck and breast being tinged with red, and shining like an amethyst. On the back of the neck is a white strip, extending two-thirds round the neck. It is even larger than the house pigeon, and is a very splendid bird.

It is found in all the forests of Europe, and is very timid and wild; yet flocks of this species breed on the tall trees of the gardens of the Tuilleries, in Paris, and being always allowed to come and go as they please, they often fly down to the patches of flowers and grass, and here the children feed them with crumbs of bread. They are almost as gentle as chickens, and it is really a very pretty sight to see these creatures diving down from the tall trees, when they see the little girls and boys throwing out crumbs for them.

THE FIRST ROBIN OF SPRING.

I AM Robin the First of the kingdom of song,
And my throne is the bough of the old cherry tree,
The zephyrs of spring bear my mandates along,
And the gentle and good are all subject to me.

Glad, glad is the home near whose precincts I stay,
A grant to abide I pay with delight;
My matin shall cheer it at close of the day,
And my vesper hymn bless it at coming of night.

As when in the gay bowers of Eden 'twas sung,
I sing to the world my melodious strain,
And the heart that is sad the earth's discords among,
May turn, with my notes, back to Eden again.

I am Robin the First of the kingdom of song,
My sceptre the power of melody sweet,
The summer's glad months my rule shall prolong,
And its flowery trophies be laid at my feet.

ISAAC'S WINTER ROBIN.

I WAS standing at my window, watching the fast-flying clouds, and the signs of a gathering storm. The ground was dry and hard, the trees were stripped of their foliage, and seemed to shiver in the cold wind. The doves scudded before it to their homes, and the fowls of the yard sought shelter in the barn. The hardy little snow-bird alone seemed to revel in the eddies of the gust, and defy the angry blustering of the storm. A whole troop of them were hopping and twittering about the gravelled walk and the lawn, as if to gather up the last seeds and crumbs, before the snow should cover them. I was pleased with their diligence, their activity, and their unanimity of sentiment, clustering together, and flying away in companies, at the slightest signal from their chief sentinel, who was always accommodated with a high place, on some adjoining knoll, stone wall, or stump.

While watching the movements of these singular little augurs, I was surprised to see a large, beautiful, red-breasted robin alight in the midst of them, and commence a diligent search for food. I had noticed a considerable piece of bread on the walk, which Clara had thrown from the window to her pet chicken in the morning. The chicken had left a portion of it; two or three snow-birds had pecked at it, and several were now trying their little bills upon what remained, when the robin, hopping briskly into the circle, seized the whole in his beak, and flew away to the woods. What could poor red-breast be doing there, so late in the season? Had he abandoned his instincts, and concluded to brave the cold of a northern winter alone, while all his tribe had followed the sun to the milder regions of the south?

Musing disconnectedly on these questions, I turned away from the window, and drew up a chair before the cheerful fire. Becoming deeply interested in my book, I did not notice how rapidly the storm had gathered, until it was howling at every door, and whistling at every window, as if it were angry to see how comfortable everything looked within, in spite of its ravings. Clara was sitting on the other side of the fire-place, deeply engaged in a splendid piece of embroidery, which had occupied her many months, and was likely to engross her time during the remainder of the winter.

"Clara," said her mother, earnestly, just as I had finished my book, "can you not afford to leave your embroidery a little while and assist me to finish these garments for poor old Jane?"

"No, mother!" replied Clara, coldly, "I can not spare the time. Besides, I do not like such coarse work."

"Do you not hear how bitterly the storm howls without, Clara? And poor Jane's cottage is not as close and warm as our house, you know; nor her woodpile as ample. Her children are actually suffering for want of these clothes, and such an evening as this should make us considerate."

Clara had set her heart upon finishing this work before her approaching birthday; and even this reasonable appeal to her benevolence did not overcome her selfish purpose sufficiently to induce her to devote an hour or two to promoting the comfort of the poor. Her mother said no more, but went on, with increasing diligence, in her work, and borrowed some hours from the night, in order to have it all ready for the morning. She hoped that a little reflection would bring Clara to a better state of feeling, and that her heart would soon respond to the appeal that had been made to it.

I was grieved to find that one so dear to me had so little sensibility—so little of the grace, which, more than any other, is the ornament of woman. I would willingly have seen her deprived at once of all her outward accomplishments, if this one grace could have been substituted in their stead; for selfishness is always and everywhere hateful, and kindness lovely in all its forms.

The morning broke clear and cold, and saw the entire surface of the country covered with a deep mantle of snow. It sparkled and glittered in the sun-beams, while myriads of shining crystals were driven here and there in the fitful eddies of the gale. The trees and shrubs were incased in crystal, and twinkled and flashed in the broad glare of day, as they waved to and fro in the wind. As I rose from the breakfast-table, I went to the window, and looked out upon the brilliant but cheerless scene. Presently, Clara came and stood by my side.

"O, father!" she exclaimed, "how I should like to have a sleigh-ride. Won't you get out the little grays this morning, and take us round the hill, and let us stop an hour at Uncle George's?"

"Yes, my dear, if you can spare the time from your embroidery."

I perceived that Clara understood me, and felt the force of my reproof, and therefore said no more. As she turned her eyes from mine toward the window, she exclaimed: "Dear father, do see this beautiful robin on the window sill!"

It was the same redbreast that I had seen the day before. I opened the window, and he hopped in upon the floor, where he busied himself with picking up the crumbs, as familiarly as if he had been brought up there; for hunger overcame his natural timidity. He was liberally provided for, and was soon satisfied; then, taking in his beak the largest piece he could find, he flew to the window again, but much to his surprise and alarm, he could not go through it. He fluttered about it for some time, and then rested upon the sill, looking eagerly out, as if longing to be away.

Though I feared the poor thing would freeze, if I let him out, I knew, also, that he would not live, if I detained him against his will. I accordingly moved gently towards the window. and threw up the sash.

After considerable fluttering, the bird found his way out, and winged his flight boldly for the distant wood.

Clara was deeply interested in all that had passed, and had many questions to ask, and many suggestions to make. "And, now, father," said she, as soon as the pretty bird was gone, "I mean to put on my India-rubbers, and fur cloak and hood, and run down to the the wood, and see if I can not find out where that robin's nest is, and what family he has there to provide for, in this inclement season."

"Well, Clara," I replied, "get yourself ready, and I will go with you."

We were soon on our way, traveling over the hard crust, as if it were a pavement of white marble. We should have found it a difficult matter, on arriving at the grove, to find the little hermit, if he had not, just as we passed the great oak, by the southern angle of the garden wall, flown up into its outmost branch, with a mouthful of grain which he had just procured from the barn. Though we saw him go up, it was still some time before we could find his refuge. At length his own motions revealed it to us. It was a nest lodged in an ample crotch, and protected from above by a third branch, which hung over it as a sort of canopy. Redbreast, while we were looking for him, had gone on another errand to the barn, and soon returned with something in his beak, which looked like a worm. Standing above the nest, he dropped the morsel, whatever it was, into the open beak of another bird, apparently as large as himself, of which, however, we could only see the head.

Determined to know the whole story of the bird whose singular conduct had awakened so deep an interest in my bosom, I procured a ladder, and ascended to the nest. Redbreast hovered anxiously about, uttering the same earnest cry as when his nest of young ones is annoyed in summer ; though he would occasionally come very near, and vary his note by one of a more encouraging tone. In the nest I found a full-grown female robin, with one foot so entangled in the strong net-work of her own little house, that she could not escape, though there was evidence that she had made most vigorous struggles to get away. She was poor and feeble, and it was a marvel to me how she could have withstood the cold of the season so long.

I believe I may say, without at all misrepresenting the truth, that the prisoner-bird, instead of screaming and struggling with alarm at my appearance, greeted my approach with a note of grateful welcome, as her deliverer. In perfect quietness she suffered me to take her in my hand, and unravel the knot that bound her, and then she laid perfectly still, while I descended the ladder, and bore her to the house, followed by her noble mate, who hovered around, fluttering from tree to tree, and from post to post, as we went. I arranged a very comfortable place for them in the barn, and redbreast soon

THE FAITHFUL BIRD MOTHER.

WHAT man e'er watched the anxious art
  Of little birds in brooding time,
That did not say within his heart,
  " God's ways are perfect as sublime ?"

The mightiest works at his behest
  Go forth in glory, bright and fair ;
And, lo ! yon little leafy nest
  Proves that the smallest are His care.

I love the Spring ! for then I see
  Young flowers all gladness and delight,
Young leaves upon the forest tree,
  Young insects taking their first flight.

I love the Spring ! for then I know
  The year its youthful course will take ;
Then, too, I view the songster go
  To build its nest in bower or brake.

Poor little bird ! how hard you earn
  A dwelling for thy infant care ;
Poor bird ! how often dost thou mourn
  Thy home, made desolate and bare :

A thousand times thy wings are spread,
  Hunger thou feel'st and loss of rest,
Ere with stern patience thou hast made
  With moss or wood, thy humble nest.

THE BIRD MOTHER.

AND when the spoiler comes! he comes
With eager haste and cunning eye,
Regardless of thy fluttering plumes,
Thy anxious arts, thy piercing cry—
O Youth! thoughtless in deed and word,
So reckless—careless in thy glee—
The Power who made that little bird
Gave life, and breath, and strength to thee

Thou'st home, and friends, and parents good,
The loved—the loving by thy side,—

The household hearth, the plenteous food,
  And all thy many wants supplied;
Whilst the poor bird the blast sustains—
  The rain—the whirlwind's bitter ire—
And when the icy winter reigns,
  It has no dwelling, food, or fire!

Thou lov'st its song, its happy song,
  It sings when summer breezes blow;
And wouldst thou seize its helpless young
  And fill its tuneful note with woe?
O! wouldst thou rend the little joy,
  The parent bliss all creatures feel?
Ah!—no!—'twere cruel, thoughtless boy,
  To wound when we've no power to heal.

The day may come—the joyous day—
  To give thy blessing to thy child;
O! were thy firstling stol'n away,
  How would thy grief be reconciled?
By memory of the rifled nest!
  The bird's lament—so like thy tone!
The anguish that contains no rest!
  The wild cry—now—now all thy own!

O Youth! forbear all treacherous arts;
  Joy, based upon another's wo,
A brief, frail pleasure but imparts—
  Man should all cruelty forego.
Praise Him, who gave thee life and light
  A home of peace, a bower of rest,
And, gazing on the poor bird's flight,
  Harm not its young, nor rob its nest!

CURED OF BIRDNESTING.

OYS generally have a fondnesss for hunting bird's nests, let me tell you how one of them got cured of this bad habit.

James lived in a pleasant village in Pennsylvania. The country around was hilly, and not more than a mile from his house was a high rock, which rose perpendicularly from the bed of a river on one side. The view from the top of this rock was very fine ; hills, rocks, and trees in every direction, with a pretty river winding through. This, of course, was the favorite resort of schoolboys in summer.

One Wednesday afternoon, school being out, James proposed to his schoolmates that they should take a ramble to this place, and it was unanimously agreed to. They started at once, with merry hearts, and the mile between them and the rock, though rather a long one, was soon left behind them. Arrived there, the party separated, and wandered off in various directions. Some exercised their dexterity in climbing trees and rocks, some sailed their little boats in the water, some hunted about for curiosities, and some others searched for birds' nests in the trees. They found but very few eggs, however, as it was late in the season for them, but found some little birds hardly large enough to fly. James was among these nest hunters, and he joined in it with as much zest as any. This was his greatest fault ; he was a fine, amiable boy in most things, and as brave as need be. His playmates were, of course, very fond of him. They did not think his fault a very serious one, as many of them were as fond of birdnesting as he was.

Just on the edge of the rock of which we have spoken, there was a sloping spot of earth. A tree had sprung up here, and was leaning over the water, that swept the base of the rock thirty or forty feet below. This spot was the only earth within the reach of the tree's roots, but farther back from the edge, the rocks rose higher, and the tree was so sit

THE BIRDLINGS.

uated, that it was watered in some degree by streams that ran down to it.

We left the boys looking for bird's eggs. Presently the egg hunters came upon this tree, and saw a bluebird fly toward it. They found she had a nest in it, just where the branches join the main trunk. They wished to climb the tree, but thought it too dangerous to attempt. James said, however, he would try it, and that eggs found in such a place would be grand trophies. The rest tried to dissuade him from it, but climb it he would. By this time the whole party were collected around the tree, and watched him with the greatest anxiety, as he began to climb. Just as he was about to put his hand on the nest, the boys called to him to come down, as the tree's roots were loosening; in another moment it fell, with him on it, down, down to the water! The treé fell a little head foremost, at first, but the head of the tree being more buoyant than the trunk, it soon floated horizontally. James, of course, accompanied the tree in its fall, and as it struck the surface a shower of water was dashed over him, and as he recovered his senses, he found himself sitting on the tree with both feet hanging in the water, and his clothes thoroughly wet. Though the current was strong, the tree was kept from floating away by some of the branches being caught in the mud on the bottom. James had not learned to swim, and there he was moored in the river with little chance of escape, the rock rising like a wall behind him and the deep water all around. His companions on the rock saw his helpless situation, but for some time could think of no way to assist him. One of them spoke of trying to find a boat somewhere along the river, but it was a lonely place, and they knew of no boat to be found. The next proposition was to make a raft, but the river banks were high and precipitous, above and below, for some distance, and few trees near it. So this plan would not do.

At last one of them thought of a long piece of rope, which he had at home. He, with some other boys, started to get it. The boys who remained spent the time looking for sticks from a foot to two feet in length—the use of which you will presently see. The boys who had gone after the rope, did not return for some time, though they went as fast as they well could. The rope was about the size of a clothes-line, but they thought it was strong enough to bear James' weight. They meant that he should climb on it, and to assist him in doing so, they doubled it together, and tied the sticks across it which had been collected, Fastening one end of their ladder at the top of the rock, they threw the other to James, who was still sitting on the tree, just in the place where it fell.

James soon got hold of the rope, and began to climb up by it. He found his strength failing him, but succeeded in reaching the top, and was helped upon the rock by his friends, who were rejoiced to see him safe. As he was very wet, he rested but a short time before he started homeward. A terrible cold followed his adventure, by which he was confined to his room for weeks.

When he recovered, he made a promise never to rob a bird's nest again—so that in the end this accident was a benefit to him, in curing him of a bad habit. If all boys who engage in birdnesting had as severe experience of it as James had, there would soon be an end of it ; and the dear little ones could enjoy themselves in peace with their young.

THE BITTERN.

THE European bittern is a very different bird from either of the species of this family in America. It is not very beautiful, and its habits are none of the neatest. Still, tastes differ; and I have no doubt but the bitterns consider themselves models among all the flying race, for beauty and propriety. The principal characteristics of the European bittern are these: General color, light, reddish yellow; upper part of the head purplish black; rest of the parts dusky; lower parts paler, with longitudinal dark marks on the neck and breast; length about two feet six inches.

This species was formerly very plentiful in England. But it is said to be rare now, in every part of Great Britain. It is sometimes seen in the less frequented marshes, where it is a permanent resident. The male makes a singular bellowing noise, not at all pleasant to human ears. The deep, guttural bellowing of the bull is more tolerable than this unearthly noise of the bittern. It is often heard at the distance of a mile, and sometimes seems as if issuing from the bottom of deep water. The nest of this bird is formed of sedges and other plants The female lays four or five eggs, of a gray colo The bird, when it rises from the earth, flies very slowly, and soon alights. Its food consists of small frogs, lizards, fishes, tadpoles, and insects.

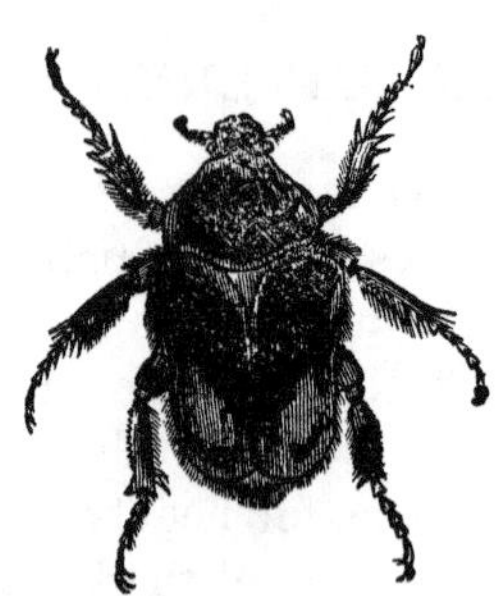

THE SPARROW AND THE FOUNDLING.

DID it ever come to your knowledge, little reader, that the sparrow, the chipping-bird as he is sometimes called, is a kind-hearted fellow, and that has been known to perform some very praiseworthy, not to say heroic acts. Well, such is the character of at least one of the members of the family, as I think you will admit when I tell you a story which I heard from a clergyman the other day. This gentleman was at dinner in a friend's house, when he noticed a sparrow fly into the room through the open door, and help himself to the crumbs which he found under the table. It appeared, too, that the confiding little fellow came and went several times, as if he was carrying food to his young. The circumstance was mentioned to the lady of the house, who said that this was a common occurrence. At every meal, regularly, this sparrow was in the habit of visiting the dining-room, and, after helping himself to a little food of carrying off some choice morsels. But the most astonishing, as well as the most affecting part of the story remains to be told. The lady pointed my friend to the threshold of the outer door, when lo! our little benevolent gleaner was feeding a young mourning dove. This bird, it appeared, was an orphan; a cruel boy had killed both her parents, and this poor foundling had no one to take care of her In this condition, she was discovered by the sparrow, who immediately adopted her as his own child, and for weeks afterward provided food for her, and taught her how to take care of herself. What a lesson in kindness is here taught us ; and how that cruel boy must have blushed with shame, if he ever heard of the care of that sparrow over his poor protégé.

THE AUSTRALIAN APTERYX.

THERE are a great many strange and funny-looking birds in the world. Some are so funny and awkward-looking, one can hardly avoid laughing at them. We wonder why they should be made to look so queer, and to move an act so clumsily. Here, now, is the Australian Apteryx, as queer a looking customer as you will find anywhere. Some of you will think, no doubt, that he has a very queer name, too—one that corresponds well with his odd shape and singular face and bill. We don't know what *Apteryx* means, but we should think such a bird with such a bill would be *apt to rip* whatever might come in its way ; and, as it has no wings to fly with, it would not be *apt to risk* getting up into a tree. However that may be, you will all agree that the fellow is not handsome—that you would not risk to have him for a pet, to be hung up in a cage in the parlor, or to be fed from your hand in the garden, Well, there is no great probability that you will ever see one. They are not found in this country. They belong to Australia, which is the name now given to New Holland, a very large island, or continent, on the south of Asia. The natives call him *kiwi-kiwi.* If that name is given to represent his song, as the names of some birds do, we should not set him down as a very musical character. We do not suppose that he indulges

THE AUSTRALIAN APTERYX.

himself much in singing. He inhabits the marshes, and lives on insects and worms, which he fishes up with his long bill.

Instead of wings, the apteryx has something like arms, or the rudiments of wings, which terminate in a sharp hook, and which seems to be intended for defence. Its feet, which are rather short, have three toes in front, with a very short one behind, the claw of which alone can be seen. It is about the size of a common hen, and of a deep brown color. It runs with rapidity. It seeks its food chiefly in the night.

THE FLOOD.

THE DOVE.

THERE was a noble ark,
Sailing o'er the waters dark,
  And wide around
Not one tall tree was seen,
Nor flower, nor leaf of green:
  All, all was drowned.

Then a soft wing was spread,
And o'er the billows dread,
  A meek dove flew;
But on that shoreless tide,
No living thing she spied
  To cheer her view;

So to the Ark she fled,
With weary, drooping head,
  To seek for rest.
Christ is the Ark, my love,
Thou art the tender dove,
  Fly to his breast.

THE MAGPIE.

THE magpie, a very handsome bird of the crow kind, is about eighteen inches in length. In color it is variegated with black and white; the black part of the plumage having (particularly on the tail feathers) a beautiful gloss of purple, green and blue; the tints changing as viewed in different lights. Magpies are found in England, France, and other temperate regions of Europe; but are comparatively rare in America, where they are only met with in the north and west. Their food is of animal or vegetable substances, indiscriminately. These birds are very familiar, and easily domesticated: they can be taught to repeat words, and even whole sentences. In their wild state, when they meet they chatter incessantly; seeming to carry on an earnest and animated conversation. They have a remarkable propensity for thieving and hoarding; and will steal not only food, but articles of which they can make no use; such as buttons, spoons, and jewelry. A tame magpie has been known to pilfer a piece of money, and hide it under the floor by dropping it through a chink or hole in one of the boards.

Their nests (which are often built in very singular places) are ingeniously constructed, with the entrance at the side. The outside is defended with a covering of sharp twigs, so interwoven as to stick out like thorns all over the surface. The inside is furnished with a thick bed of wool, or of any soft substance they can mat together.

We have seen an anecdote of a lady in England losing an expensive lace cap, which (with other articles of a similar description) had been spread on a grass plat to bleach or whiten, after washing. The cap mysteriously disappeared, and was supposed to have been stolen: but there was no ground to fix suspicion on any person in particular. A few weeks afterwards, a magpie's nest was discovered in one of the garden trees, and in the nest was found the lace cap, which had been pulled to pieces by the bird and formed into a sort of mattrass for her young ones.

The famous story of the Magpie and the Maid, is said to be founded on fact. The Italian version of it is far more striking than the French; though the latter is the one most generally known, and has afforded a subject for a play and an opera.

According to the Italian account, there is a tradition in Florence, that a lady of that city on returning one night from a ball, having taken off her jewels, laid them on her toilet-table, and retired to rest, leaving the windows open on account of the heat of the weather. Being much fatigued, she did not awaken till a late hour next morning, and she then found that her pearl necklace was missing. The ornament was of great price, and she suspected it to have been purloined by her waiting-maid, who was the only person that had entered the apartment while the lady was asleep. The girl in vain protested her innocence. The laws of that country and period were always rigidly enforced on those who had neither wealth nor power to screen themselves from punishment, whether merited or otherwise. The unfortunate girl was imprisoned, tried, and being unable to clear herself of the suspected crime, was sentenced to death for the theft. On her way to the scaffold, there came up a sudden and violent thunder-storm. In front of the muncipal hall, and near the place of execution, stood a statue of the goddess of Justice, holding in one hand a sword and in the other a balance or pair of scales. A flash of lightning struck the balance from the hand of the figure, and when it fell to the ground there was found in one of the scales a magpie's nest, containing the identical pearl necklace for which the poor girl was about to suffer death. Her innocence being now manifested, she was restored to the favor of her mistress; and her sufferings were repaid by unlimited confidence in her integrity, and numerous acts of kindness and munificence.

THE CORMORANT.

IS web-footed, and dives for its prey, which it swallows voraciously. An eel will sometimes, by wriggling and struggling, almost release itself from the engulfing throat of the cormorant, then the cormorant arouses and swallows *again*, till the eel is captured and dined upon at the same instant, and dies among the digestive organs.

The eggs of the cormorant are laid upon a flat rock, near the water. It is easily tamed, and its fishing propensities turned to good account. The Chinese employ them in this way, placing a ring around the neck, to prevent their swallowing the fish.

THE BIRD BATTLE.

One bright summer morn I had wandered away,
  By the din of the city beset,
And found an abode near whose precincts all day,
  Scenes of beauty and grandeur were met.
Quite tranquil I sat in an arbor at rest,
  And gazed on a glittering wreath
Which hung like a crown on the near mountain's crest,
  The landscape wide spreading beneath.

Far down in the distance a white-sailed sloop lav
  Like a gull on the water asleep;
Abreast of the headland it held on its way,
  But seemed as if chained to the deep.
All nature was lulled in a languid repose;
  The birds were too listless for song;
E'en the clouds seemed preparing their eyelids to close,
  While the river lapsed idly along.

When all of a sudden I heard such a scream
  Burst forth from a neighboring tree,
As speedily banished my half-finished dream,
  And made a close watcher of me.
A robin and blue-bird, engaged bill to bill,
  In sanguine encounter I saw;
They fluttered and clattered and hacked away, till
  I thought they must blood largely draw.

Now red-breast was topmost—he cuffed and he kicked
  The little blue-wing right and left;
Then blue-bird did head of cock-robin afflict,
  Till he seemed of his top-knot bereft.
I shouted to stay them, demanding a truce,
  The cause of the feud while I gained;
I offered to mediate—what was the use;
  No audience could be obtained.

THE BIRD BATTLE.

A contest was raging, and had to be lost,
  by one or the other, be sure;
A victory gotten, at whatever cost,
  Naught else could their heart-burning cure.
I ceased intervening to watch the event,
  With patience becoming the case,
The blows fell less rapid, but seemed far from spent,
  Each foeman subsiding apace.

When down came the big drops, loud sounded the boom
  Of the thunder-storm sheeting the skies;
Away shot the robin far into the gloom,
  Away fled the blue-bird likewise.
The noise of the conflict was instantly drowned,
  The combatants nowhere were seen.
The rain seemed determined such things to confound,
  For it poured forth a deluge, I ween.

No sign did I witness again of the birds,
  Though the shower was presently done,
They failed to rekindle, in notes or in words,
  The battle which neither had won.
What lessons, I pondered, might here be well learned,
  For curing an outbreak or broil,
In cities misguided or e'en overturned,
  By factions in love with the spoil.

A shower's the thing, but of water, not ball,
  Well applied to the top of the head,
To banish the qualms of law-questioners all,
  And make them law-lovers instead.
Then let us remember, when riots are rife,
  And fighting is getting too free,
The readiest method to settle such strife,
  Is, to treat it *hydraulically*

YOUNG BIRDS AND CHILDREN.

WELL, there is not so much difference between young birds and children as folks might suppose. One is a young animal on two legs, *with* feathers, the other a young animal on two legs *without* feathers. That is about the distinction, as we hold. Perhaps the microscope applied to the cutaneous covering of the latter animal might reveal embryo feathers, at least, if not embryo wings, *a la spirituelle*. We can't say much for the wings of either of them, to be sure, for the wings of the young birds look for all the world like Connecticut pegs—shoe pegs—all in a row, which have suddenly taken the fancy to blossom at the ends, and as for the folded wings of the veritable cherub, we suppose they are hid in the wrinkles of fat which prevails over the best specimens of premium babies!

We do not fancy metaphysics in treating of plain subjects, however, and therefore as we consider young birds extremely ugly, we will not undertake to gainsay that phraseology in speaking of babies. The fact is, if we are candid, the bird and baby are alike, little fatty monstrosites, stuck all over with ridiculous pin-feathers, looking particularly wicked and bare by way of contrast, we suppose, with the horrible red flesh underneath them. They both have wide mouths, always agape, and specially ogreish, pale, hungry eyes. They both look faint and solemn, as if they were sick and sorry that they had ever come into the world, and hold a suspicious expression of doubt as to whether there is food enough in the world to keep them in it, which expressions give a certain degree of mournfulness to their aspects that is truly confounding. They seem to feel as if they had been inveigled, by some unaccountable treachery, into an arid existence, in which both food and drink were so scarce that they must both be taken " on the snap !"

Yet, when the little monster flares wide the blue clefts of inward life upon her vigil, she sees again the same hungry questioning of doubt. It seems to say, What have you got? What have you got? Can I live in this drear space? What wonder the poor mother is terrified! What wonder that she shudders at the thought—this being lives through me — I am Earth, Heaven, the Universe to it! Should the lacteal founts within me fail, then must it go away! To this being, at least, I am divinity! She has not even the comfort of the mother-bird, that trembling mother! She can not think of the myriad forms of bug, and worm, of fly, and seed; she can not remember where countless insects lie in hordes to feed her gaping babes. The fruitfulness of a fecundant earth does not rise up before her vision, nor does she know that every leaf is the abounding platter from which her young may be fed; that every root, and herb, and unturned pebble has yet its secret store, which she may search in boundless confidence.

Yes, the little bird-babies are god-mothered by

tub of Diogenes roll, clittering with the pearly click of a low laughter.

Did you ever see a young bird attack its first bug? Well, now, you have got something to learn and to know of fun in the world, till you have seen that sight! He first gets behind his mother to peep at the black, many-legged, and crawling monster, from beneath her tail. She picks it up and gives it a toss against the ground, with a *nonchalant* air to give him confidence. But no, the little staring wise-acre is not to be taken in. That thing looks too begrimed and ugly, not to be wicked, he's certain. So he stands on tiptoe, and stretches his half-bare neck, hugs his meagre feathers to his side, till he looks as if he could slide through the eye of a needle, spreads his stumpy tail, and with head awry, and eye wide-spread, inspects the monster with a serene caution, from a distance. The impatient mother gives it another toss, and this time throws it fiercely against the ground. Our little hero begins to think that looks like fun, and so he stoutly dashes at the foe. But when he feels the writhing of its shell-like leg against his bill, he dashes it from him as if it had been a live coal, and makes a pretty, flitting leap into the air.

Poor bug! he kicks and writhes upon his back, and birdie, crouched behind his mother, stretches his neck to an unreasonable length, and stares.

The impatient mother now gives the bug a good pounding, until she breaks its shell-casing against a pebble or a root, and it lies with gossamer wings protruding from the clefts, all stark and stiff beneath her feet. Now youngling becomes suddenly courageous, he marches towards the bug with slow, progressive hops; when, in its dying throes, one leg

is stretched out, quivering. Away Sir Valiant hops, with a sharp chirp of affright! and grows longer and smaller still with this stretched compression of his cautious fright.

The mother gazes on him with a cool, dissatisfied air, and suddenly plumes her wing as if the scene we used to know of more than fifty nests which we used to take a cautious peep into, once a day, for we never ventured to touch them.

Suddenly, to our great consternation, we perceived that nest after nest had been robbed! And many a lovely dream of pleasant play-fellows was dissipated in rapid succession. We were sadly bewildered for the cause, and finally came to the conclusion that all the bad and vagabond darkies of the neighborhood must be dogging our steps, and, watching us when we peeped in at our dainty treasures, came immediately when we disappeared, and carried them off.

At last the sidelong appearance of the nests, thus robbed, attracted our attention. We began to wonder why it should be, in all cases, that the robber should *tip* the nest. And then there were no tracks of human feet about. At length we found a nest, with a clear round hole through the bottom of it, and the eggs all abstracted; and we forthwith swore vengeance against all snakes.

The next day we marched forth with gun in hand, and the painful cries of a pair of sparrows, whose secrets we knew, attracted our attention, and we went forthwith to ascertain the cause of their troubles. As we approached the nest, we saw a huge black snake, glide glistening away in the clear morning sunlight. The thieving scamp, when he saw us approaching, reared his head aloft for battle; but in a twinkling it was taken clean off with a rifle bullet—and then the poor brooding birds of all the neighborhood had a temporary "surcease of sorrow."

Well, we had been watching for weeks, the doings of a splendid pair of cardinal grossbeaks, or Virginia red-birds. Their family arrangements had been twice broken up by his snakeship ; and now the gay attire and clarion note of the flashing male bird, soon betrayed to us the site of their third house.

We found it in a little arbor of wild grape-vines, in which we had said prophetically, early in the spring, "some bird will be sure to build." We watched the cosy pair daily from a distance, and counted the hours, until we were sure the young ones *must* be fledged.

The day on which the time was up found us peering curiously into the grape-vine. But the old birds had almost been too sharp for us. On that very morning, two of the young had been coaxed entirely away from the nest, and the other perched cosily among the broad foliage of the vine. The gentleman of the vine looked as wise as Minerva's owl, and we are impressed with the belief that he really was ; for, instead of attempting to get away, he stepped gingerly upon our wife's dainty finger, and crouched himself down upon it to get warm.

We liked this for a philosophical beginning of an intimacy, and "Captain Red," as he was forthwith christened, became at once a "high particular." The other young one, which was a female, and the weakest in the nest, soon died. But "Captain

Red" flourished apace, and soon became quite as much a gentleman of estate, as ever poor artist or naturalist could be!

He peered into all our correspondence, and picked at the letters of our MS. until we are convinced that he became quite as conversant with our affairs as we were ourselves. We are quite positive that this gentleman of the top-knot was, and is, quite as wise as anybody of his day and generation.

Now, we will tell you why. All that part of the world, which is wise and good, does its thinking through the heart; and so did "Capain Red," as you will see from our narrative.

We took up a strange passion for the little wood-wren, which is found all through the West, with his nut-brown and black-barred mantle, and white streak above his eyes. He is the most incorrigible music-box in existence. He sings always. Frost and snow have no power to chill the warm pulsation of his little organ; and, sunshine in, or sunshine out, he persistently shrills a clear accordance, that defies all thought of despondency or grief. His liquid pipe, rollics and rings among the bare trunks of winter, defying its discords, as well as melts in shrilly clamors with the breezy flush of spring.

It is, in a word, one of the most charming and indefatigable songsters we have in America, and the quaintest citizen of the peopled woods withal. He has a remarkably cunning way of hiding his nest, too, in old hollow trees and stumps, and in decaying logs, in odd fence-corners, and perforated eaves.

Well, with all its cunning, we managed, after long and patient watching, to find a nest of these young gentry, just in their fledging time. They are very rebellious little scamps, and we got them home, with much trouble at first, and placed them in the house of " Captain Red," and oh, it would have done you good to see how promptly our quaint philosopher, though only six weeks old himself, took up the cause of these transplanted little ones!

He at once assumed the airs of maternity, fraternity rather, and seemed to be immensely puzzled and vexed, that the little obstinate wretches would not eat seeds, which seemed to him to be the natural food of all birds. After trying for several hours to make them eat the seeds, which he so carefully masticated for them in advance, and stuffed into their gaping mouths, only to see it rejected with a toss of contempt, he seemed to come to the conclusion, that they were nothing but heathen, anyhow ; and seeing that we fed them with worms, which he did not eat, he came to the conclusion, that they must live anyhow ; and he therefore masticated for them most daintily the repulsive things! which he fed to them with an air of disgusted resignation, which was absolutely irresistible.

Many a shout of laughter have we indulged in, in watching the resigned air with which the philanthropic little fellow would cram their throats with the nauseous food. Yet he wore all the time an amusingly hopeful air, as if he expected gradually to reform the little barbarians, and teach them that seed constituted the only legitimate food for civilized birds.

To our no little sorrow, our friend "Captain Red" succeeded. The little fellows came to be convicted that they really were barbarians! And the imitative scamps soon took to the use of seeds as the staple of life! So they commenced eating food which they had neither bills formed to crack, nor stomachs formed to digest. We tried in vain to prevent this, but "Captain Red" resented it as an interference with his prerogative, and continued to stuff them until all our interesting little pets died of indigestion, and we found their craws filled with unbroken seeds.

THE TURKEY CHASE.

ARLY in the spring, we left the city, and went to live on a farm. The first time we visited the old people who owned the place, was on the most dismal day you can imagine. We started to walk over from the residence of Mrs. E——, but before we had walked half the distance we became so numbed from cold, that we finally stopped in the woods, and built a little fire of the dead twigs and leaves, to warm our feet. Ough! how the wind blew! How chill the half foggy half rainy air seemed, and as we climbed the steep hill sides, we had to cling to each other, to keep old Boreas from fairly whirling us away in his brawny arms. The trees cracked as they bent, groaning beneath the wind, and the dead leaves danced frantically, high and low, in circles, and in sudden dartings forward in straight lines, now seeking shelter in crevices of gray rocks, or hollows of dead trees. But in vain, for the ruthless wind followed and drove them forth again, until perhaps they sank into the half-frozen pond in the valley.

But we had determined to overcome all difficulties, and battling with cold, wind, and damp ground, we finally reached Mr. R——'s residence, and, not finding a gate, commenced climbing the fence. At that moment a mulatto woman came out of a cabin in the yard ; merely glancing at us, she proceeded to hang up some wet clothes, which she took from a basket, upon the line.

"Hallo! is your mistress at home?" said Mr. W——. But the girl appeared not to observe that she was spoken to.

"She must be deaf," said C——.

By the time we had reached the ground on her side of the fence, however, the girl came hastily forward, and with her chin stretched out, and her ear a little inclined towards him, said to Mr. W——.

"My ole Miss gone visitin', but ole Massa at home, sir. Go right in that way," pointing towards a door at one end of the house.

The house was a large one, and quite new. Indeed it had been so lately furnished that the old people were scarcely settled in it yet ; and so fine a house was it, that all the neighbors were saying, "What in the world can those old people want of such a great house, at their age? Why, they will scarcely live long enough to get settled in it! If they had children, one could understand it. But they have nobody to care for, but their negroes! How strange!"

Well, well, we had been told to go into the door at the end of the house ; in the meantime, the girl, or "Pop" as the old man called her, had given him warning that "folks comin'," and he met us at the door. We were soon rapidly thawing before a large wood fire, and while the old gentleman was hurrying about, getting us something warm to eat and drink—as the fashion is in Kentucky—we told him our errand.

As soon as we had lunched, we were shown over the house. The old gentleman, evidently very much gratified at our admiration of it; said he had no doubt but that his "old woman" would like to have us come, and advised us to select the room we liked best, promising to let us know the old lady's mind on the subject next day. Accordingly a room with three large French windows was chosen. Looking from the south window, we had a broad stretch of green fields, dotted, away yonder, with farm houses. From the east, the lane stretching from the front yard down to the wood which bordered the farm, in nearly every direction. West, more woodland, and the cabins of the negroes; a portico, in front, completed the attractions, except the two fine locust trees under the south window.

The, old lady's consent was quickly given, when she discovered that I liked chickens and young turkeys, and we were soon installed in our new quarters.

The peculiarity which first struck us in our new location was the crowing, cackling, and gobbling of the most astonishing number of fowls we had ever seen collected before. It was positively wonderful, the clatter the cocks made every night at twelve o'clock, and in the morning at day-break; we really could scarcely sleep for them at first, and although the old lady had some three hundred hens on the place, it was the most amusing thing to find that she never sold either eggs or chickens, but kept them all, through the sheer love of such pets.

Another amusing thing was to observe the old lady, with the consternation of a veritable old hen,

THE CHASE.

herself, rushing hither and thither about the yard, followed by her train of little "darkies," to collect her forty or fifty broods of chicks, and house them all before a threatened rain. Many a time have we stood at the window, laughing heartily to see the sturdy old dame, in her dire tribulation, with the mingled rain and perspiration pouring from her wrinkled cheeks, rushing up and down, screaming to her worthless "darkies," and frightening the poor old hens, with their clittering broods, almost to death, in her eagerness to save them from the weather.

Such a busy time as there was on these occasions! What between the violent clucking of the old hens, an occasional battle between them and their over anxious mistress, the cries of the young ones, the universal crowing of the cocks, the cranking of the great flock of geese, the phut, phut, of the astonished turkeys, the squeaking of the dismayed pigs, the bleating of the sheep and calves, the neighing of the horses, and the hisses of the old drakes, the vociferous screamings of the blind old grandmother negro, hurrying up the indolent young ones to the assistance of their mistress, the mournful howlings of the dogs, who always joined their voices in any general clamor, and we have a time worth being witnessed by any children brought up in cities.

There were other funny things which caused us great amusement too. We sat up very late one night engaged in writing, when the air of the room become oppressive, the window, before which our lamp was burning, was thrown open, and it happened to be on the side west the barnyard. Instantly there was a general burst of crowing, from the throat of every chanticleer on t place. The effect was quite astounding; at first it was impossible for us to conceive "what could the matter be," and looking at the time, we found it was not near twelve o'clock, and as all the geese, and turkeys, too, on the place, joined the general hubbub, we could only conclude, after listening quite puzzled for awhile, that all the multitude of feathered people on the place had mistaken the light of our lamp through the window, for that of the breaking day. We afterwards amused ourselves by repeating the experiment, and after obtaining several hearty laughs at the expense of their simplicity, we found that if they did wear feathers, they were not to be fooled too often, for they soon ceased to crow at the sight of the light.

Another very curious fact, which we observed in relation to the habits of domestic fowls, was that the flock of geese were perpetually walking round and round the house, in single file, the live-long night, until twelve o'clock. Look out what time you might, from the window into the dark, we could see the head of the single file of white forms make its appearance round the corner of the house, and on they would stream, in dead silence, like a funeral procession of white ghosts, or head-stones that had taken to gadding. As they never uttered a single sound, and as you could not even hear the pattering of their soft splay feet upon the grass, the effect through the dim shades of the night was extremely quaint.

During the whole time of our stay, this thing was repeated every night; and you may imagine how curious it was to watch the procession regularly at the instant when the cocks crew for midnight, gravely squat themselves on one particular spot, and remain there till daylight, silent and motionless as death.

This habit of domestic geese affords quite a remarkable example of tenacity with which the usages of the wild varieties from which they are originally descended, are retained even after many centuries of domestication. It is well known to all observers of their habits, that the wild geese on their migrations, fly until twelve o'clock at night, and then descend to rest and sleep until morning. They are found at daybreak alighted and feeding on the fields over which they have been flying. Even when not migrating, they are known to be feeding busily until midnight, from which time they sleep.

It is a fact, we believe not to have been as yet commented upon in books of natural history, that all domestic creatures, which are descended from the migratory tribes, exhibit invariably an extraordinary restlessness when the period has arrived at which their wild kinsmen migrate. We will give you several other curious illustrations of this fact, in our succeeding stories, concerning the habits of our pet birds.

But before we dismiss this account of the habits of domestic birds, it may be as well to relate to you a most affecting and interesting incident, which we witnessed in the habits of the domestic turkey.

It may not be familiar to all our little readers, that those persons who are in the habit of raising fowls, who are most successful, are accustomed to notice, with great care, the habits of the hens of the different breeds. Those which prove themselves the most motherly and careful, are quickly selected out, and the eggs of all the careless mothers, as well as their own, placed under them to hatch. Because, you may rest assured, there is just as much difference between the hen-mothers, as between the human-mothers in this respect.

So that on one occasion, while visiting our sister in south Kentucky, we found one of these motherly turkey mother-hens, at the head of a brood of about thirty young, who had by this time grown up to be quite as large as their mother, and quite fit for the table. So one night, our sister ordered the old black cook to select from the roosting places of the flock, a fine fat young gobbler, and despatch him, on the occasion of a grand dinner we were to have on the next day.

The cruel old cook performed her task, as many negroes do, without caring whether she was right or wrong. The next morning, to our inconceivable astonishment, the whole twenty-nine remaining turkeys, old gobbler and all, came under the low window of our sister's sitting-room, and as long as they could see any member of the family through it, kept up such a clatter of clucking and plaintive cries, as were probably never heard before, from the same number of turkeys. It was a most singular scene indeed. They were gathered together in a cluster, marching back and forth, passing and re-passing each other, the females uttering the most plaintive cries, while the males, sometimes joining them in their clattering cluck, would then suddenly droop their wings, and with fiery heads and hanging wattles, utter a simultaneous shout of angry gobbling, such as was almost defeaning.

The moment they would lose sight of the members of the family through the window, they would set off round the house, in procession, and the moment they saw any one, such a gobbling, gobbling yell, and clutter! This seemed the more astonishing, as this same flock of turkeys had never been known to remain near the house before as late as sunrise, but were generally, by that time, a mile off foraging through the meadows, for grasshoppers and crickets.

We immediately suspected that there must be something wrong; there was an expression of reproach, so unmistakable, in the cries of the poor creatures, and something so unaccountable in their conduct, for they literally besieged the doors and windows and seemed with their timid, yet despairing looks, to be pleading with us for some precious soul, or life.

This scene had been kept up for several hours, and had become so painful to us all, at last, that we determined to ascertain the cause, if possible. We went out into the kitchen, and asked to see the turkey that had been killed over night, when we found to our infinite sorrow and pain, that the cruel old cook, had carelessly chopped off the head of the *Mother* of this flock, instead of doing, as she had been directed.

We never were more pained by any similar incident. Poor creatures, their plaintive and persistent cries, were now explained. They had lost their good mother! She by whom they had always been led, " through the green meadows, by the cool waters." Ah, you may rest assured, that there were at least two pair of eyes, that were not very dry when we made this sad discovery! And you may rest assured, that not one mouthful of that turkey did we touch, during that great dinner.

There was something terribly human in the reproachful entreaties, with which they continued to assail even the dinner hour for the rescue of their mother, so much so, indeed, that the turkey was not touched. No one could find it in his heart to eat it —and " little Nannie " cried at its being brought on to the table even. Ah, it makes one sad indeed to think how much of cruelty is committed in the world, by mistake or carelessness, even when not intended!

But we will return to the farm again. In all probability we shall meet the old lady as we climb the steep hill sides. For at least once every day, she takes a stick in her hand, ties her linen kerchief over her cap, and in her thick carpet-shoes, tramps down the lane to the cliffs. For what think you? Why, those troublesome turkeys of hers will build their nest in the crevices of the rocks. They prefer the shady nooks and corners, they find there, to the snug barrels and little houses, which the old lady is always preparing for them, up at the roosting place. It was very droll to watch the cautious movements of the mistress, as she approached a group composed of one bedraggled hen, attended by two or three lordly gobblers. Each of the parties watching jealously the slightest movements of the others. The hen, who has a fine nest in a well-hidden spot, yonder among the rocks, walks slowly and with an indifferent air, to all appearance, here and there, and picking daintily at this, or that, but always with her eyes looking askance for an opportunity to run! At the moment she fancies she can escape, see what a sudden bustle! A moment before those turkey gobblers were strutting before her, their heads furiously red, their wattles blazing like rainbows, their wings stiffened and scraping the ground, their tails trailing, their eyes glancing upward, and their whole air, that of the most absolute, self-congratulation!

Madame, the sly hen, suddenly darts off, her head lowered, her body pinched in, as if she would make her progress more rapid by offering less surface to the atmosphere. The gallants stand a moment, astonished! then, all at once, with wings furled, tails lifted, heads suddenly diminished, and with gobble! gobble! of displeasure, pell mell, after the wilful lady. What does she mean? does she wish to deprive herself their worshipful company? ungrateful! But she pauses again, and with an expression, which is as plain as words could be, says to them, "What's the matter with you all?" and begins to pick and watch again, while they, seeming to fancy that they have been unnecessarily alarmed, display new graces to enchant her. The old lady gravely resumes her hiding place behind a tree—from which she too had darted, when the panic was at the highest—and waits with the most suprising patience on the tactics of the hen.

Sometimes she waits for hours before the hen can escape her admirers, and stealthily reach her nest. When at last her patience is rewarded, she follows to the nest, seizes the tenant by the legs, bears her in triumph to the nest *she* has prepared for her, and comes panting in to the house to report the trials she has encountered. Towards sundown, a new expedition was generally on hand. The young turkeys had been led off by their mother to the wheat field, and "dear me! Liza! Mary! come here, you lazy children, and help me drive up those young turkeys!" was the cry, and then, such trials! all over the great field, with its heavy grain obstructing every step, would the old lady trudge while "Liza and Mary," would sit down behind the fence, on the grain to rest, laughing because they were playing, while the old "misses" was plodding tediously and patiently around the field.

Her treasures all housed, at last, the old lady would seat herself before the fire, and, with knitting in hand, repeat to us the many, many trials, she had had that eventful day with her chickens, her turkeys, her geese, her goslings, and last, not least, those lazy negroes, who had given her more trouble than all the rest.

STORY OF THE THREE GEESE.

WE had from the first noticed in the great flock, that went trailing so solemnly round and round our house, every night, a very handsome female; indeed, by far the handsomest goose of them all. We had observed also, that while nearly all the other lady geese had regularly paired off, and were each accompanied by a separate lord, this handsome one was always attended by two gallants.

As geese are very faithful to each other when they are paired, we were not a little surprised at this, especially when we perceived that there were several females, who always kept together, who had no mates at all. In a short time the handsome lady went to setting; and as she was the first of the flock who did so, all the eggs which had yet been laid were placed under her.

As the little barrel-nest, in which she sat brooding, lay in front of our window, we had constant opportunities of observing her. You may not be aware that, in all the wild, as well as tame, varieties of this bird, when the female commences brooding, the male takes up his station, as sentinel on guard, beside her nest, which he never leaves beyond a discreet distance, from whence the spot is in full view, that he may protect her in her interesting office, from all intrusive foxes, minks, dogs, cats, or what not, that may approach her.

Swans will even attack men, under such circumstances, without hesitation; and so great is the courage and vigor of their assaults, that they have been known to break a man's arm, short off, with a single blow of the butt or shoulder of their powerful wing.

We would not, therefore, have been surprised to see one gander on duty, at his post of guardianship, but we must confess we were surprised to see two. The same two we had observed escorting her about; each jealous of the other, but equally vigilant. The largest and strongest of the two held the place of honor, close by her side, while the other occupied a position some three feet off. He never attempted to come an inch nearer, but that the stronger one instantly assailed him. And what seemed very curious, although this constant warfare was, and had been constantly, going on between these rivals, when any intruder approached the nest, they both charged at the same instant upon it, and together drove it off.

It was very quaint to watch madame, during

these scenes ; with what a demure expression she seemed to regard the joint exertions of her rival friends, on her behalf. She looked on with such an innocent air of placid sweetness, that it was enough to make a frosty Zeno laugh. What could it mean ? It was clear that she was not the wife of both !—for neither polygamy nor bigamy is practised among these tribes. And from their simple and undeviating faith, in ragard to their connubial relation, mankind might take, in these corrupt days, from the "silly goose," a most important lesson.

What then could it mean ? Was this some unnatural deviation from a general truth, or law ? We had ascertained, beyond any doubt, that this was impossible. We will see if we cannot satisfactorily account for this interesting phenomenon.

In due time, madame, "the beauty," hatched out an amazing brood of little goslings. First the admiration and wonder of her two friends excited our mirth ; but afterwards, when the whole surprising miracle, of the entire new battalion of little furzy yellow balls went rolling and staggering about the yard, the amazement of the entire flock of grown geese was too absurdly ludicrous to be fitly described.

As soon as the announcement of the new arrival had spread, they marched up to the scene, in phalanx, with stately waddling gait, their necks all slim in stretching wonder, their reddish goggle eyes looking as if they would burst from their heads. They formed in a circle, at a respectful distance; for when one of the little strangers would stagger towards them, they would scatter and run with an expression of stolid wonder, that would have made you shake your sides to witness.

We do wonder what they thought the little monsters were? The curiosity remained unabated several days. They would follow them about, in procession, wherever they went, and so eager did they become at last, to examine them more closely, that the two champions of "Lady-beauty" found great ado to keep them at a respectful distance, and prevent the young from being trampled to death, with their great, splay, awkward feet. The third or fourth day, the general flock seemed to have settled in their minds what these little strangers were, and they accordingly ceased to persecute them with their curiosity.

THE THREE GEESE.

During all this time, it was interesting and even touching to observe the untiring solicitude of "Lady beauty's" conquered suitor. Now we could see the group of three—the conquered gander holding always the same relative position that we have seen before. He never came any nearer the female than the privileged distance of three feet, off to one side, and a little in the rear, always keeping a vigilant look-out lest any of the little ones should fall too far behind—always ready to hurry it along, when its tired legs sank under it, and the panting ball of yellow down crouched itself in the crisp grass to rest. Or if, in its ambitious emulation, it rolled over, in the attempt to pluck a blade of grass too tough for his soft bill, and strength, then this watchful gander was sure to be near to lend a helping foot, or bill, to push him up to his weak feet again. He seemed even more attentive to these babies, than his favored rival. For many a time, when the large gander unmercifully walked over them, in his eargerness to march side by side with his lady, this patient fellow would stay behind, and, allay the panic. Now the secret of all this is so touching, that we are sure that no little one, who reads this story of The Three Geese, will ever be found persecuting or throwing stones at these simple creatures. We had begun to suspect what the real story was, and after prosecuting the most vigilant inquiries into the history of the group, found out exactly how matters were.

It seemed that "Lady-beauty" and the hindmost gander were both young people, and at pairing time, this young gallant made violent love to the recognized beauty of the flock. But, an older gander than he—a stronger—the tyrannical master and leader of the flock, had taken a fancy to her also, he having lost his own wife by some accident.

He accordingly laid claim to her, and at once there ensued a series of battles — of which their broken feathers still showed the marks—between the two, which at length became so desperate that the mistress of the "Famous Farm" was compelled to separate them — placing one in confinement. When he was released the battles re-commenced, raging with even greater fury than before ; for the younger, though worsted in each contest by the snperior strength of his rival, still continued the conflict, whenever they met in the presence of the beauty they both coveted.

Things continued in this way until the younger one was nearly killed, and the mistress was obliged to confine him several weeks. When released, he found his rival fairly paired to the "beauty," and he seemed to give up the struggle. But his heart was too faithful to permit him to lose sight of her he loved, and having relinquished all claim to her in every other sense, he would not give up the humble privilege of being near her, of seeing her, and of helping her to protect her young, and serving in any humble but faithful office.

Now this is a simple but literal story of humble fidelity in a goose, that shames the thousand high-flying and silly romances of human passion and affection. It is true every word of it—for we watched them faithfully, through the whole season, and when we left the "Famous Farm" late in the year, precisely the same relation continued to exist between the three.

The little man who reads this, will never throw stones at a poor goose again, and imagine that he has not a heart to be wounded and a body to be hurt!

One more fact about geese before we close, and they are wild geese, this time. It is a very interesting incident to old children as well as young, and reveals a characteristic not much known, especially in the north.

Some eight or ten years ago, a rich gentleman, a farmer, who is called Colonel Robert Scott, and lives about sixteen miles north of Frankfort, Kentucky, on the Lexington railroad, was walking about his extensive premises very early one morning, when he observed a solitary wild goose, swimming hurriedly back and forth in a beautiful little fresh water pond, not far from his house. Supposing it would fly away, and being a good-hearted man, not disposed to injure wild creatures, he continued his stroll, and the inspection of his affairs.

Presently, to his surprise, his attention was attracted by a violent fluttering in the lake. He perceived to his sorrow, that the goose which was making agonizing efforts to rise from the water, must be severely wounded. For exert itself as it might, there was one wing which refused to do duty. Some reckless sportsman had evidently wronged it, that is, broken a joint of a wing, and it had tumbled headlong into the pond, from its ærial voyage.

It was terribly frightened, as it well might be, at the sight of man, and besides, as it could get no food, was in danger of starvation. The good man's compassion was touched at the miserable plight of the stranger, and instantly issued orders that no one was, under any pretext, to trouble or frighten it, and from that day he regularly strewed the corn for it along the edges of the lake with his own hand, and this being continued the whole winter, by the time spring came there had gradually grown up a sort of intimacy between the amiable colonel and his crippled protegé.

After a while thė loud craunk! craunk! of his natural friends, returning from the bleak winter of the Arctic and Canada, towards the South, struck upon the ear of the solitary bird, and turning his eye aloft, the long V like line of which probably he had so often been the apex and the leader, were visible, floating high upon the journeying winds.

Instantly, loud cries of welcome resounded from the surface of the lake. There was an instantaneous pause of hesitancy, in the high-away lines, and the leader, fluttering from the steady beat of travel, wheeled on his broad wings about, followed by his double train.

The cries of the solitary bird alone, were redoubled, with yet more conch-like resonance, and all doubt above, seemed to be at an end. It was the cry of a friend, which called down the travelers, and sweeping in broad gyrations, down and down they came, uttering clamorous cries of greeting, until, with a few short flappings, as they neared the surface, the whole flock was launched upon its clear waters.

Surrounding their long-lost friend, such sonorous clamors of delight were never heard in that quiet region, before. After several minutes, when the first eager explanations were over, such splashing and diving, as there was, would have done your heart good to see. Even the poor prisoner, scarce knowing what he was about, in his bewildered joy, splashed, and washed, and dived, too, as eagerly as if he had just come from a flight across the world.

The good farmer Scott, who witnessed the incident, was immensely pleased that his poor friend had at last met with his own people, and had probably heard pleasant news from that rush-home in fenny Labrador, over which he had so long grieved. He determined at once to offer them every attraction; so that an abundant supply of corn was thrown down.

The thing was so well managed that although, in a short time, the great body of the flock, moved on, in their southern way, greatly refreshed by such generous hospitality, a few of the weaker or younger birds, we suppose, stayed behind to avail themselves of it—remaining the year round, as if to keep the old bird company.

With the next spring, there were additions to the flock which came in the same way, and the colonists began to thrive apace, breeding upon the shores of the little lake, in undisturbed security. So the thing went on from year to year, until, when we last heard from this interesting flock, a year ago, it numbered about three hundred individuals, and it was a sight so interesting, to see the fine old Colonel scattering his buckets of corn, in the early morming, with all his three hundred pensioners, crowding and craunking around him, that people came from many miles to witness the sight, and it has now become one of the notorities of the neighborhood of Frankfort.

This is probably the only instance on record, of any extended success, in taming these wild and hunted denizens of air.

quick they are! Now, do not let him go. I would not lose him for a kingdom!

All this time the silver triangle was rapidly ringing with furious earnest on all sides; first, on the top of this mulberry; then, yonder, the other side of the fence; then down the valley; now up on the hill-side; the whole wood seemed to have suddenly been filled with a troop of mad fairies, who were calling to arms, all the quaint people of earth, air, and water, to the rescue!

"Will it sting?" was the very natural question we asked, as we timorously held out our hands to receive the mystery!

"O, no!" laughed Mr. W.; "but, here I will put it under my hat!" and he put his hand to his head, which made me laugh, too; for I knew where his hat had gone, while he was chasing that "something." "Well, lend me yours, then!" and quickly my hat lay on the ground, and "something" was under it, while I was sent to pick up some pebbles to keep the hat down.

"Well, then, what is it?" I asked.

"Look up, there, upon the first twig of that great maple, that stands close to the fence! Do you see that wee bundle of brown feathers? That is it? That is one of those little scamps, that have so dexterously managed to get out of our reach! That is his father and mother making all that ringing fuss! and they are the very little wood-wrens we were so anxious to get a peep at, all last year!"

O, how delighted I was! We had one under my hat; but that, Mr. W. said, was a female; we must have that young gentleman in the tree. He was the oldest bird. The only one that knew how to climb in the nest, out of seven or eight; he alone had clambered, or half flown, into this very secure place, as he, no doubt, thought it. And, in fact, he was not far from the truth; for my eyes had not yet been fully able to discover whether there was a knot, or a bird, on the twig.

But Mr. W.'s eyes were too keen, and too well accustomed to the habits of birds, to be mistaken. He bade me watch the little fellow, while he had another search for the bird under the rail. After a minute, Mr. W. sprang to his feet, exclaiming: "Catch that bird! close to you, running towards the spring!"

I sprang forward; there was a dainty birdie, scarcely larger than a butterfly, spreading its little wings, and running as fast as it could towards a heap of brushwood, which the rains had swept together. I caught him in the folds of my dress, and then took a peep at him. Such a beautiful little creature as it was, in its plumes of soft brown, marked with faint black bars, a line of creamy white over its bright dark eyes, and its figure, so trim, and like some veritable wood-sprite.

We placed him beneath the hat, with his little sister, and then began to think how we should reach the gentleman on the twig, which was at least thirty feet from the ground; to climb it, was out of the question; and if we threw at it, we might hurt it. The question became a serious one. How could we get him? There he sat; not a feather moving; a perfect monument of patience; watching us, but believing himself well hid. The old birds, in the meantime, had ceased their clatter, and were, I suppose, watching our dilemma with great satisfaction. But we were not going to be baffled. At last, Mr. W., who was all eagerness, exclaimed—

"Ah, I have it! I will outwit that cunning youngster!" and running to a clump of tall marsh willows which stood near, with nothing but a small pocket knife to help him, soon cut down a pole of nearly twenty feet in length, which tapered to a delicate point, which could not hurt the little one, if it should touch him. Then, clambering to the top of a high fence, which touched the tree, he directed me to keep a sharp look-out below.

With delicate care he now raised the point, with which he could barely reach the fugitive, and with a soft push, soon dislodged him. Down he came, fluttering like a little butterfly, to the ground. I, who had been standing on a pebble in the little stream, darted forward to the cry: "Be quick! be quick! Don't let him get up a tree, for he can climb like a little squirrel!" and sure enough, the active scamp was already climbing the trunk of a huge tree, when I reached it, and compelled him to take to the ground again, where he was soon hid beneath a rock.

The old birds were by this time ringing their metallic ter-r-rer again ; and now we could see them flitting about the rock, under which their little one crouched, seeming to fancy that now, at least, he was safe from our clutches. But this was a prize not to be so easily given up ; we pried away the stone and captured him. The old birds now instantly flew away, and commenced peering into all sorts of odd places, which served to convince us that they had at least, five or six more nestlings left.

Hurrying home with our prizes, we quickly ascertained that two out of the three were females, the last captive being the only vigorous bird we had. This would not do at all ; we must have a pair of these dear little birds, which we were likely to raise. We might never again have so fine an opportunity for obtaining the young of these creatures. They were so adroit in hiding their nests, deep, within the hollows of prostrate trees, or, as in this case, amidst the brush and stones, which had been swept down the valley by the winter rains. They were so cautious in introducing their young families to the dangers of the great world, and the little ones learned so quickly to protect themselves, that we had better accept this happy chance, which threw into our way these lovely birds, whose wild, clear, shrilly song had penetrated our hearts with its melody, long before our eyes had known the wee fairy form of the darling.

Often in the winter, while in South Kentucky, when all other songs had long since ceased, in the evening, when the sun was yet warm and glowing, from the topmost bough of some solitary tree or post, would suddenly ring out its brilliant notes—clear, loud, sweet, and thrilling, seeming most like the keen refraction of the sunshine, glinting, through ice drops on the trees, cheering the senses chilled to numbness, by the bleak December. Never could we get a glimpse of this mysterious little songster, who thus came to make our hearts glad, thus make the dull winter joyous, and glow in the brilliant summer, his gay heart held. But Mr. W. knew his family well, and we had faith that we should see and make friends with this merry musician yet.

All the spring, too, we had been puzzled by a brilliant song, which we thought must be that of this wren, down in the valley. It had a familiar tone, but we could never see the bird, or hear any notes which we remembered to be precisely identical with those we had heard before. To be sure, the bird must be a phantom—some wizard bird, who could never be seen by mortal; who grew silent, if you approached his perch, and was a dream to all nature; whose notes were silver arrows swiftly darting through the air, penetrating it with a keen and sudden splendor, which made all other sounds pause and fade, until the woods seemed sleeping, or breathless, by waiting, to be again surprised.

THE WRENS AND THE ORIOLE.

OW that we had three of the so much coveted wood-wrens in our possession, we hastened home with our treasure, and after feeding the obstinate little scamps, we placed them in a little basket lined with soft stuffs, and covered with green gauze, to prevent them from injuring themselves in their efforts to escape; then we took a hasty meal, and concluded to return immediately to the scene of our late adventure, with the view of capturing others of the brood.

How this was practicable I could not divine, for I naturally supposed they would take themselves far enough away before we could get back. But Mr. W., from his knowledge of the habits of this family of birds, explained: "No, it is not likely that they endeavor to escape from the neighborhood of that immediate spot, for the young birds having concealed themselves among the great rocks and fallen timber around, the old birds who know where each one is hid, will consider them more safe where they are, rather than venture for the present upon what they have just proven to be the dangerous open ground ; and besides, they are close to the nest to which they will have to return, for some time yet, for shelter, as night approaches."

So we hurried off, taking with us the little basket containing our captives, whose cries would soon attract the attention of the old birds, when, if we sat still patiently for a while, having them once under our eye, we could see them coming to feed each of their scattered little ones, in their different places of refuge.

It was a cruel device, to be sure. But those who would instruct others in the habits of the natural world, must capture its creatures for the purpose of studying its habits more perfectly. We tell you these things, not to instruct you in cunning stratagems, that you may indulge in wanton cruelty toward these beautiful and innocent beings, but to show you how affectionate and intelligent they are, that your sympathies may be aroused to protect, rather than to outrage them.

Well, we soon arrived at the spring, with its little stream, and the deep gorge down which it tumbled in successive tiny cataracts. We sat ourselves down upon the mossy stones, and looking round, for some time there was not a living thing visible.

At the first cry, however, of our little captives, the brave and watchful mother, who had no doubt been gliding round us all the time, silent as some shadow of brown Elfin of the rocks, suddenly sounded her sivery t'chir-r-r, t'chir-r-r of alarm, and darted quickly, and ringing by us, and perching for an instant on a point of rock near us, bounded from side to side, with stooping breast, and pert tail cocked over head, and scolded us at a great rate, after the most quaint and impish manner; while the male, just over head, in the most vociferous style, sang out, as swinging half-way round a twig, he hung with head awry, and small waspish eye peering down upon us.

But it seemed that such was the little sinner's irreverent love of music, that seeing no overt mischief going on, he darted upward from twig to twig, till he reached the top of the tree, and burst forth into such a strain of brilliant notes that our hearts were moved, and we would surely have let the little captives go, but that Mr. W. said, "No, it can not be; we must study the habits of this little bird. It is painful, but there are many such painful things to be done by those who would glean new facts from nature."

The female continued to scold us for a little while longer, and with such accents of indignation that we could not help feeling a little guilty, although we knew that what we were doing was a duty, and not an act of idle cruelty; and then she flitted away down the valley, and all was silent as death again.

We now watched for a considerable time in the direction in which she flew away, without seeing any movement. At length, when our patience was almost worn out, Mr. W. whispered, "Hist! there she is! see her silently leaping from root to stone! She has a bug in her mouth! Now we have her secret! She comes to feed one of them, and will reveal its hiding-place."

So, after many cautious evolutions, we saw her disappear beneath a shelving rock, from which she soon emerged without anything in her bill.

"Now for it! we will have that youngster, anyhow!" and we rushed forward to the spot, when, to our dismay, we found there was quite a cave underneath the overhanging rock; and when we knelt for a better view, we could only peer into a distance far too deep and black for *our* arms to reach the bottom of it. We were puzzled for a moment.

"Never mind! with all their cunning," said Mr. W., "they are silly little fellows at last; reach me that long stick—and you, place yourself there, where the upper surface of the cave slopes down to within an inch or so of the bottom. I think I can drive him out into the folds of your dress; I don't think he has gumption enough to know when he is safe; but you must be quick."

After a deal of poking into the deep recesses of the cave, without success, we were about to give it up as a desperate undertaking, and sat consulting what to do next, when who should pop out but our lovely, little brown imp, with his creamy breast, and pure white streak above his brilliant, little soft black eyes.

He looked so innocent, that he had evidently just come out to see if all was right, intending, if the coast was clear, to find some other quarters, where there were no such ugly noises. One spring and we had him!

This fresh capture seemed to cause dire consternation among the old folks, and almost immediately we saw the mother, who had darted to the hiding-place of another close at hand, which she seemed to think not sufficiently secure under these new assaults.

She came forth, leading him away with great rapidity. We hurried in pursuit, and such a chase as we had of it! We thought we had our hands on him half a dozen times, but he "was not there," and it was not till after many doublings and turnings, that we succeeded in capturing the quick and dextrous creature.

We ascertained in the same way that there was another little one, concealed, as we supposed, in or near a huge hollow log which had fallen across the ravine. After sounding the hollow in all directions, and searching on every side half an hour, we found the little simpleton at last had been squatting all the time in a pile of loose stones a few feet off, from which he made his appearance of his own accord, as we supposed, to look after our movements.

Here was another exciting and helter-skelter chase, before we succeeded in capturing him also. We now had six of the young, and as these would be amply sufficient for our purpose, we determined to leave the other two as some consolation to the poor parents for their loss, and turned homeward more purely delighted with our treasures, than if we had picked up six peerless diamonds of the finest water.

As we neared the house, "Polly," the mulatto girl, came running forth to meet us, holding some small dark object in her hand.

"Here, miss, here!" she exclaimed. "Here's a little bird for you? Uncle Alek picked it up in the yard jes now!"

UNCLE ALEK'S PRIZE.

We took it from her hands, when lo! what should it be? A beautiful male orchard oriole! or "hang-bird," as the country people call it, its splendid coat of purple and brown glistening in the spring sunshine, and its dark eyes vivid with untamed life.

We were as much astonished as rejoiced.

How could this have happened? The bird did not seem to be sick, or to have been hurt. We asked "Polly."

'Don't know, miss ; ole Uncle Alek say he ben a fightin'!"

"Well, but what have you been doing to him? Here, he has grease on him!"

"Why, miss," laughed Polly, "de children ben tryin' to feed him wid de hog fat."

"Why, Polly! Polly! Polly! what could you mean by letting the children stuff this dainty creature with hog's fat?"

"Why, miss, we don't know what he eat?"

Poor creature! What barbarians it must have thought it had fallen among. All away from amid the fruits and flowers of the tropic South, fallen in the weariness of flight, or beaten down in some premature battle with a rival foe, to find itself prisoner in the hands of rude negro children, who attempt to stuff its delicate throat with villainous hog's fat! That throat, which had as yet drank only of the dews distilled from heaven, and gushed only the joyous music of love, amid perfumed airs, and the rustle of soft green leaves. Pooh! faugh! the very idea! How we caressed the beautiful stranger! and in our double joy at the acquisition, and in having been enabled to rescue him from such hard usage, we almost, for the moment, forgot our little wrens.

We hurried up to our room, and the first instinct, of course, was to rid it, as far as could be gently done, of the base greases with which its shiny bead and musical throat had been profaned—and gently, ah, how gently, did we handle it—this far-comer of a beaming land! It had been silent heretofore—had uttered no cry, nor made any attempt to escape. The negro had rolled it passively into our palm—and we had wondered that, full of life as it seemed, it made no attempt to spring away into the free air, when it would have been so easy.

But now, when those horrible black forms, with their greasy pork, were gone, and it was held with caressing gentleness in the hand, it commenced to utter the most plaintive, the most strange, and pleasing cries. Oh, how touching they were! Half joyous, as if for its relief, and liquid, rich, and plaining, as if demanding, in a higher tongue, the self-same boon of higher intelligences than those from which it had just been rescued.

It did not seem to be either passive now with fright, or disposed to struggle to get away, but only uttered its clear, harmonious call at rapid intervals. We soon perceived that the little creature was very lean, and it struck us that it must be most weak from hunger.

We had already prepared a paste of crushed crickets and grasshoppers, which, carefully dried in the sun, could be at any time, after being soaked in new milk, used as food for young birds. Dipping a common camel's hair water-color brush, of medium size, in this diluted paste, we have always found that upon applying it gently to the bill of a bird, whether young or old, they would be more readily induced to feed than by any other method.

We now tried this experiment with our new friend, when he ate with an avidity which proved him to have been in reality nearly half famished, and soon perceived that between each interval he uttered his sweet call with clear joyance.

Poor little weary wanderer! how pleasant it was to see him grow warm and glad, and meet his clear look, growing more and more confiding as he saw we offered him only pleasant things, and gave him no vile pork.

And when at last we came to place him in the roomy cage, he bounded to and fro, with wagging tail; and ah, you can not tell what delicious reward it was to us, when, at cock-crow in the morning, we were awakened by the wild and fluent melody ringing in our ears, close to the bedside.

How gay and shy the little fellow seemed! He had a rival, too, on the locust tree, just outside that window, and such a sweet vociferation, strain for strain, as they kept up, answering each other, until the sun rose. We lay as if in dreaming we listened to the dream-land music, and all the big house became reverberate of sounds. We thought it might have been in contest with this very rival on the locust tree that our bright friend had fallen exhausted, to be captured by old Alek.

We had observed a shy and modest plumed madame "Orie" for a day or two before, gliding, fidgeting, among the young leaves of this same locust, and we had concluded that there would be a nest there in good time. We used to stand to one side, half concealed by the curtains, and watch her as she came out to the very ends of the limbs—some of which were within reach of our hands—and anxiously peering in through the glass at us, as if to satisfy herself whether we were likely to be quiet neighbors; and we had taken very good care to make no movement that would have a tendency to startle her good opinion.

For, most of all, it was a delight to us, the idea that we should be enabled, from such close neighborhood, to witness the whole wonderful process of the nest-building of these birds, who, you must know, weave and sew their hanging cradle with all the skill of human artists; and then the thought, too, that we should see the little eggs come, one by one, so mysteriously, and watch, on the sly, the endearing scenes of love-making; and then when the time arrived for incubation, to listen to the soft twittering gratitude of the brooding female, when her faithful mate came to bring her food; and then, to listen to the love-song, with which he gaily soothed her weary hours—you cannot think what a prospect of pleasantness these anticipations had afforded us from the first signs of her purpose to make her summer home in this tree.

Now, we felt certain that since she had heard the gay song of one of her own species from within this dim room, which she clearly regarded with so much suspicion, she would be decided to settle there.

We had already attempted to lure a pair of merry blue-birds, with the same view, who were evidently seeking a locality also, by placing a gourd, with a hole in it, on this tree, opposite our window; but we saw that after a few sharp, decisive battles, the male oriole had triumphed, and the discomfited blue-birds flitted to and fro, still merrily disconsolate, looking for a home, with which we soon afterwards supplied them, in the shape of a nice little box on the next tree, where we could readily command their every movement.

Our little wrens were, for a few hours, very obstinate. They would neither stay in the warm nest we made for them in the basket, nor take any food, unless we took them into our hands, and opened their mouths for them. We had emptied a large box, and placed their basket within it. We gave them an opportunity for running about, and hoped they would soon be hungry enough to listen to reason, and accept us for parents.

But they had to be coaxed. Finally, almost in despair, we recollected that Beckstein—the German bird tamer, who has written so much about the management of pet birds—says, if a quill is used, young birds may be induced to eat without the danger of injuring their bills. Now, the bills of these little ones were soft as flowerbuds, and we had been only able to open them by passing our long finger-nail delicately between the mandibles, and compelling the youngling to open its mouth with the slight pressure we made.

Instantly, we thought of our water-coloring brushes. Selecting one of the swan's quill size, dipping it into the mixture we had made, of crushed crickets and grasshoppers, soaked in new milk, we applied it gently to the mouth of one of the now sleepy birdlings. The titillating at the base of the bill made him gape his yellow mouth, and we dexterously dropped the wet brush within it.

It evidently pleased his palate, for his eyes flew open wide ; and as we offered the brush again, the mouth was gaping to receive it. Here was a triumph. After all our efforts, the brush had achieved all we desired, for the gratified twitterings of this little one had roused the others, and they, too, were soon clamerous for a share.

From that time, they hailed the approach of our hand as the signal that the brush was coming with a new supply of food ; and it was very quaint to see this group of little birds running about the box, their wings spread, their tails thrown over their backs, and those dainty mouths of theirs stretched wide in clamorous eagerness for food, food, food, every time the green vail, which covered their box, was lifted, and the brush appeared.

The food we gave them was very nourishing, and they grew apace; but by an accident, three of our little treasures were killed. Do not ask me how, for I do not like to narrate such sad events. The other three were soon too impatient of imprisonment to stay in the box, and as we had become pretty well acquainted with each other, in a day or two we permitted them to play about us in our room. Then commenced their antics—such funny, wee things as they were. They were so babyish, they did not know anything in the world but the brush. They knew that, but did not know why it refused to give them food when our hand was not at the other end of it. They would seize it, one at one end, another at the other, bite and tug at it, drag it about the room, under the chairs, tables, bed, anywhere and everywhere, while the third would follow, squalling, beseeching, with eager, upturned bill, but all to no purpose. The brush was obstinate, and after a hearty laugh, we would capture the brush, and while all three of the baby-birds were on tip-toe with expectation, all begging at the same moment, and watching the movements of the brush with impatient expectation, we would dip the unkind representative of mother-bird, and restore their faith in it in a moment.

Then away they would scamper—play with the

most surprising energy for about fifteen minutes, and then one after the other would clamber into our lap, and, hid away together in the folds of our dress, sleep a little while—a very little while, however, for we could scarcely say, "They are fast asleep," before first one, then another, would withdraw his head from beneath his wing, stretch a wing or a leg, hop upon our knee, and then with a chirp spring off for a new frolic.

We had to teach them to bathe. When we first put them into the little bath-tub, with about an eighth of an inch of water, with the chill slightly taken off, you would have laughed. Standing on tip-toe, with wings slightly elevated, neck stretched to its utmost length, head inclined, and eyes gazing into the mystery, they seemed utterly to fail in the comprehension of it. We could not help laughing merrily. We had to throw the water over them repeatedly, before we could make them understand that it was solemn earnest, or that it was a new duty which they were to learn. And even when they had learned this much, it took them a long time to find out the process of drying themselves, as their mother had done before them; and how to teach them puzzled us a good deal—we had no feathers to shake, no wings to spread, and bill to smooth feathers with. We did what we could, however. We gesticulated as vehemently as possible, we talked as rapidly, we shook our heads and hands, we doubtless astonished them. We shook their little wings as softly as we could—and it all ended with a hop, jump, from our shoulder to our puffed hair, and a soft whispering, as they nestled close to our ear, swinging in this new cradle.

Or if the hair was not properly arranged for them, then there was Mrs, W.'s sleeve, or mine, or the collar of Mr. W.'s coat, under his voluminous hair. They would nestle and twitter, and in a moment would be fast asleep; and no matter how much we moved about, our motions were to them quite as natural as the swinging of branches in the woods would be.

Of course we had to present the wrens to our friend Orie. They had made inquisitive visits to his cage, peering in at him, and evidently very anxious to make his acquaintance. Accordingly, we opened Orie's front-door, and in walked the three little baby-birds. Master Orie was astonished, you may be sure, at the invasion. He flew to the top-perch in his cage, stooping over, and watching the manners of the intruders below.

They were staring about, looking for all the world like simpletons who had suddenly been transplanted from a wilderness to a palace. Such lofty bars, such long perches, such heaps of dinner, such huge baths; all was wonderful! But their marvel soon took a new direction. Little natives as they were, every thing must be examined, and to work accordingly they went. "Bob" had taken it into his head to pursue Orie, and from perch to perch, and from top to bottom he hopped, determined to find out the meaning of his superior size, the difference in his color, and his excessive shyness.

Orie patiently evaded him, waiting, on the stoop for fresh flight, every advance the young gentleman made. "Mouse" had quietly taken possession of the large bath, and was soberly regarding the effect of his legs as he stood immersed to the tips of his wings. "Lady" was busily engaged in overhauling "Master Orie's" pantry. Presently, when Orie grew hungry, he descended from his perch, and then what a picture! All these baby-birds, these naughty little scamps of intruders, gathered about him, entreating and squalling, begging and hopping about him, while Orie, poor fellow! stood staring from one to the other, on tip-toe with surprise, and uncertain what next to expect from this obstreperous troup.

They soon found that they entreated in vain. Orie continued to regard them, first with astonishment, afterward with indifferent disdain. Yet they paid him one or two visits daily. We sometimes amused ourselves by shutting the door of the cage, and then watching the efforts they made to get out after they had grown tired of the cage. Their impatience was funny, and it always had the same result. Out they came, how, it was difficult to understand; but after squeezing and scolding, pushing out a head, a wing, a leg, drawing back again and trying another space, they always managed to slip through the bars.

One day the windows were all open, the birds were playing about the room merry as bees, talking to each other, full of all sorts of antics. The brush had been made to perambulate the whole surface of the floor, when a sudden pause, a stillness in the room startled us. We looked up from our drawing. "'Bob, Bob!' 'Mouse!' 'Lady,' where are you? Come here quick," said we, as we commenced peering about the room after them.

"Mouse" and "Lady" instantly presented them selves, but "Bob" was invisible.

We at once conjectured that "Bob" had made an exit from the window, and after a hasty search about the room, we ran down into the yard, calling "Bob, Bob!" and whistling the sound which he was accustomed to reply to, when we wanted to feed him. We had the brush in our hand, and had full faith that if he but caught a glimpse of us or it, or could hear us call, we should again capture the runaway.

We ran hurriedly to and fro. As we came under the locusts, Mrs. W. exclaimed, "There he is!" and almost before the words were uttered "Bob" had sailed down with unsteady flight, and stood panting on my shoulder.

Poor little "Bob!" He was sadly terrified. There, in the tree above him, still darting about, were the two orioles we told you about in our last

was with them (and at all events his would grow), were infinitely amusing.

Our birds were very fond of the warm fire. They would play about it for hours, and while they were warm enough, they would not get too close ; but if the fire burned low, and they no longer felt the glow upon the floor, then they would gradually draw closer and closer. We did not know what to do with them. They would not stay in the cage, and we feared they would be killed some time when we were out, by flying into the hot ashes.

We finally got a long, slender stick, and every time they approached the fire, we would make such a racket with it on the floor between them and the fire, that they would dart away in grand consternation. We finally succeeded in making the stick so much a bug-bear, that we had only to place it in the corner, and they took good care after one or two efforts to conciliate it, never to go too near to it ; and in this way we saved them from burned toes, if not some greater misfortune.

We are very fond of wild flowers. We await the appearnce of the first timid blossom with great eagerness, and there are few nooks in the woods that we have not at least peered into. Indeed, wild flowers and young birds hold a wide space in our heart. Thus, then, we never fail to have flowers in our room when there are any to be found ; and our friends are all so well aware of our fondness for flowers, that we often have them long before other people dream that they have arrived.

Orie's cage we had carefully kept supplied with green branches, grasses, and wild flowers, and on the top of the cage we had a vase filled every day with some kind of flowers and vine-leaves. These bouquets were not pyramidal in form either, by any manner of means, but rather assumed the quaint and graceful forms which nature presents to us out of doors.

Under this bouquet, "Bob," "Mouse," and "Lady" loved to play, chasing each other round and round, under the roses, over the vines, now mounted on the top of the vase, now crouching amid the clusters of green leaves, playing bo-peep with each other or us. And here the three baby-birds made their day-cradle. Often, when all grew still in the room, when the cheery sounds our pets made were all silenced, and we looked up to see what it meant, we would see Orie almost nodding on his perch, while gathered together, a little handful of living feathers, breathing softly, as if a new-born wind-spirit animated them, and bearing no semblance to bird-form, we would find those dear nestlings cosily sleeping, a rose for a canopy, flower petals for a couch, and the shadow of fresh green leaves for cradle-curtains.

Then, in our deep love for them, which was always growing, we would take the dainty treasures gently with our hand, lifting them all at the same time, and, placing them in the palm of the other, watch their soft slumber; and how strange it seemed! Those sweet birdies had so learned to know our presence, our touch, that they would never be startled. They kept their heads beneath their wings, and the only token they gave was, that they nestled more closely together, and murmured a fairly-like melody of loving sounds, too exquisite for any human to imitate.

Then when the twilight came, and our treasures grew impatient for their nest, then we made them a soft bed in their basket, and placed it beside our pillow, anticipating the early calls for "brush," "brush!" the loving caressess and droll antics in the morning, when at the first peep of light into their basket they came scrambling out, to hop upon our forehead, or warm themselves in our hair, or in our bosom.

We told you how we came to call one of our wrens "Bob," but we did not tell you why the other two were called "Mouse" and "Lady." We will tell you at once.

"Mouse" was a male bird, but, unlike "Bob," who was a gay, noisy fellow, his motions were smooth, gliding, and noiseless, and he had a fashion of finding all the sunny nooks and corners. If there was any fold in my dress, which formed a particularly cosy shelter, "Mouse" was sure to find it. He had first made the discovery that our ears were warm, and that our hair was the very best material for a comfortable swing.

He made another discovery also. Our window-curtains were knotted together in the center of the broad windows, forming many large folds. One day we heard an unusual talking among the little folks. "Bob," and "Lady"—who had received her name on account of her womanish ways, and for the attentions the others paid her—were peering, stooping, and tip-toeing, twittering, and now and then giving us the full benefit of that silvery triangle of theirs, while at the same time their expression was that of birds extremely puzzled.

"Mouse" was invisible, but we could hear him, calling with low, gentle whisperings, now a little louder, now almost lost, as if the little fellow was going to sleep, but was still endeavoring to keep himself awake long enough to let his friends know where he was.

We followed the sound after listening a minute, and found "Mouse" safely stowed away within a deep fold of the curtain close to the knot, where the gathering together of the two sides of the curtain made a great many folds, and, of course, formed a shady, warm nest for the young gentleman.

When we gently parted the folds above his head and looked in, he turned his bright eye up to us, and nestled more snugly down in his new-found napping-place, while the two others flew down from the top of the bedstead, and gazing in at "Mouse" instantly perceived the justice of his selection, the value of the discovery, and without any further ado. plunged into these new quarters, where, after pushing and crowding, and fitting the cradle to their wee-bit forms, they twittered approval, and went to sleep. After this, for some time, whenever we returned from our long walks, we would be sure to find our babies in their curtain-bed, waiting our return ; and the moment we approached it, before we had yet looked in, they would recognize our presence, and greet us in their dainty way.

It was strange, too, how quickly these pets would comprehend the characters of people who came to see us. Sometimes they would scold, and scold, at persons, and we could not induce them to go near them. When other persons came, they would play about them as they did with us—*never* dreaming, apparently, that people could hurt them—but only some people were not as good as others. And it usually turned out to be true, that those very people whom the wrens disliked, were vicious, impure, or in some way untrue. One day, the old lady at the "Famous Farm" had a party of children to visit her. Several of them came up to our room to see our birds ; among them were two little girls, one about eleven years of age, the other about nine. The oldest girl could not make friends with them at all. They squalled at her, flew off to the highest furniture in the room, and she had finally to go away without having made the first step to win their favor.

Presently the younger girl came in. In less than five minutes the birds had flown down ; one was on her head, another on her shoulder pulling her ear-rings ; the third was pecking something from her fingers. While the little girl was perfectly delighted at her conquest of these very fastidious young citizens, she played with them several hours, they seeming to consider her nothing more or less than another bird, introducing her to all their secrets, brush and all!

After a long frolic, the birds grew sleepy, and as the little girl sat in a low chair, one after the other settled themselves in her lap for a nap. They were very tired and were soon sound asleep. The little

girl sat still as a mouse for a long time, when suddenly she whispered, "See Mrs. W., these dear little birds all sleep in the same position, their heads all turned the same way! and every time one changes its position all the others do. Are they not pretty?"

And indeed they were pretty, their light-brown backs shining in the same rays of light, their heads hid under their right wings, and so tiny, soft, and still, that I did not wonder at her exclamation and admiration of them. Besides, how tame they were! She constantly caressed them, passing her little fingers over their feathers, patting and whispering to them while they slept.

In the same way they treated our friend B., how came sometimes to see us and them. He loved the little birds, and they seemed to love him, and thus they always continued to make distinctions between people.

I have not time to tell you, in this paper, all the many droll and pleasant things in the lives of our pet wrens. Of their antics, at their first introduction to a cricket, or a locust, their subsequent valor in the attack of the liveliest of all the insects we found for them, when, after long rambles and hunts for bugs under logs, tearing away the dead bark from fallen trunks of trees, lifting stones and digging into the earth after spiders, etc., we returned with all sorts of treasures of food for them; or how they learned the use of the dry sand-bath, which we prepared for them, and how they would bask in the sunshine as they lay in the sand, tossing it over their backs, sifting it through and through their feathers; and even their wonder and timid play, when we took them into the woods or fields with us, and let them run about. Ah, that was a pretty sight! They seemed to think the world so large, and bare, and full of strange gigantic forms, and they would gaze about them, and then run to us for protection; and when we showed them bugs, out-doors, they were always half afraid, unless we sat down upon the ground by them, while they conquered and devoured them.

All these things we must pass hastily over, or we shall never tell you all we most want to tell you about them, or our other pets.

One fantastic caper, however, we must tell you. We had made a collection of rare young birds—little, little things—too small to have any but pin-feathers and down upon their bodies. And they were such ugly things, with fat bodies, some kinds looking like balls of yellow butter; some purple, looking like ripe plums; some red; and but for their mouths, which were beautiful, and when they stretched themselves up in their several nests—which we kept together in the same open basket—and all at the same moment, their wide mouths bloomed—we seemed to have suddenly had placed before us a little parterre of rare wild flowers, instead of those ungainly forms—and then the odor which their little lungs poured through the throats of those blossoms was as rare as they.

We have often raised birds from this age, so that you need not be surprised that we should have taken birds so young from their mothers, for you will recollect that it was always our purpose to understand all about them, from the beginning.

But to return. The appearance of these little birds, or monsters, as the wrens evidently thought them, seemed to excite much astonishment, considerable jealousy, and a firm determination on the part of the three pets not to be superseded by these participants of our care. If we fed the young strangers, then in an instant we had "Bob," "Mouse," and "Lady" mounted on the edge of the basket, their wings lifted higher than those of the birds below, their necks stretched longer, their mouths wide as possible, and their stronger lungs making all the noise they could, so as to compel us to feed them first; which we were half the time obliged to do to get rid of them.

And to be sure, rid we were of their clamors, to be astonished at the coolness with which first one, then another, would quietly drop himself into a nest, crowd aside the young ones, and have snugly surrounded himself by their hot, fat bodies, tuck his head beneath his wing, just keeping one eye slightly open, to judge of the effect his impudence would have upon us, or the innocent owners of the nest, who, of course, were too unconscious to comprehend what was going on, while we had to scold and laugh and protect the poor little things.

One day we had occasion to open our portfolio to seek a drawing of ours. The birds were as usual playing about us. We had, by the way, thrown our portfolio open upon the bed, and commenced throwing out the drawings, soon covering the bed with them. The wrens thought this fine fun ; they were hopping over the papers, bounding up at every unusually loud crackling of them, dragging one sheet here to the edge of the bed, and dropping it over to see it float off, diving under others, running through some rolls of paper which lay there, too ; in short, perfectly mad with the new excitement.

Suddenly—tchir-r-r-r ! tchir-r-r-r ! tchir-r-r-r ! rang out the silver twang of that invisible triangle ! We looked up. There mounted on the tip-top angle of our large pillow, stood Master "Bob," his eyes wide open as they could be, his head flattened like a snake's, his stump of a tail over his back, his body presenting first one side, and then the other as he, with a jerking swing of the body upon the pivot of the toes, lowered his breast at every swing and sang out, with an air of intense excitement, that metallic tchir-r-r-r !

The other two were equally agitated. "Lady" had gathered her dark feathers together, and crouching or tip-toeing behind "Bob," who was her favored admirer, she added her more than mite to the furor which "Bob" was making. "Mouse," at the other end of the bed, was doing his very best to outdo him, and, for a moment or two, I was completely at a loss to know the meaning of this sudden outbreak.

When our voice joined the clamor, "Bob" came down with a bounce, toward the center of the bed; then halting suddenly, vociferating in the most extraordinary manner, his body thrown backward, while he was fairly tip-toe with excitement!

We now saw what was the cause of the tumult. A colored drawing, representing a thrush, lay there, slightly elevated at one corner. I withdrew it from the others, and stood it up against a pillow. "Bob" followed, screaming, while the other two squalled, and watched the result, for it now became very evident that there was a skirmish on hand.

After several times nerving himself to the attack, and each time retreating, at the very "tug of war," "Bob" made a dash—pecked at the very extreme tip of the painted thrush's wing! Back again! Again! For a moment "Bob" stood and stared—his squalls ceased—the cries of the others grew faint, like dying echoes!

Again! This time the bill of the thrush was the mark! What! *no* resistance? "Bob" nearly pitched sideways with astound! leaning his full weight on the right leg and foot, while the other foot scarce touched the bed. Again he attacks! *This* time in faith, with a plunge, enough to annihilate even a paper bird; the mark is the eye!

"Mouse" and "Lady" have descended, and

stand eagerly watching—uttering at intervals their tchir-r-r-r, but with an undecided emphasis! "Bob" makes one other advance—this time slowly; he stands confronting this thrush. "He does not resist yet, hey—well, then," said "Bob's manner, "he is *no* bird! I disdain any further knowledge of him!" and he turned his back upon him, while "Lady" continued yet some time to scrutinize this semblance and "Mouse" ran behind the paper, pecked at the edges, stood on tip-toe beside it, perched on the top of it, and finally, also came to the conclusion that it was a humbug!

Mr. W. went away for a few days about this time, and before he started bade me take good care of the "little folks" which I promised to do, you may rest assured, for we had grown to love them dearly. In a day or two after his departure, I started to go to the post-office, which was about two miles and a half distance.

I say, started. For some reason I could not bear the idea of leaving my room. I had a feeling that some unfortunate event was about to occur. What could it be? My birds were perfectly well—never gayer and more endearing than this morning; every window was shut, they could not escape! nothing could reach them in shape of cat, or other vicious enemy. What then? At last I went on, feeling sad, but determined to hasten back as soon as I could.

On my return toward home I found a number of

their favorite bugs, etc., and had quite a budget of rarities for them, and had besides almost reasoned myself out of the idea of danger to them. Arrived, I hastened to my room. All was silent. "Dear birdies, come down and see what I have brought you. Come, 'Bob!' 'Mouse!' 'Lady!'"

"Mouse" came, slowly and alone. I showed him the ant's eggs, the crickets, green grasshoppers, and all the other nice things I had brought, thinking as I continued to call, that the two hid-away little darlings could not long resist his exclamations of wonder, joy, and eager appreciation of what I had brought.

Nobody came, however.. I became alarmed. I commenced to look for them. At length "Lady" stretched her head over the edge of the bed-tester, and at my repeated entreaties came down to my hand. But where was "Bob!" I called, I searched in all the cradles. No "Bob!" No "Bob!" I was on the point of running down stairs to ask who had seen him, when oh! oh! my poor bird, my darling little hero! he lay before me on the writing-table, still, *so* still! his attitude natural, no appearance of convulsion—only as if he had dropped in flight across the room, and died in an instant! He was scarcely cold! He must have died just before I came into the room!

The next morning poor little "Lady" died too! She came into the bed, and nestled close to my cheek, ah, so lovingly, her little weary heart was nearly broken. She had come to me for sympathy. She talked to me in whispered, slow melody; she asked for her friend "Bob."

When "Mouse" came hopping across my forehead and breast to seek shelter from the solitude, she would start up with a cry so piteous, that my heart ached.

Once, when this happened, she fell back as if she was dead. I sprang up, and threw water upon her breast. She recovered then, and I held her till she was dry and warm again, caressing her and hoping she would take comfort in the love I gave her. At last, while I was dressing, she flew toward me, suddenly, and dropped at my feet, dead!

I will not dwell longer upon these sad events. Enough, that my last wren, poor "Mouse," turned to us for consolation. We took him with us wherever we went. He was our constant companion, out-doors and in. He was sad and lonely, and we pitied him with our whole heart. Orie and he were great friends. But Orie was too old a companion for "Mouse."

One morning, three or four days after "Bob" and "Lady" went away, "Mouse" was playing on the window-sill, and a troop of hemp-birds settled on the locust tree. They coaxed him a long time to join them, and after many parting glances at us, and many returns, he went off with them.

Orie's cage-door was generally open. *This* morning it was open, and Orie silently departed also, leaving us alone! We were deeply grieved, but we could not be so cruel as to restrain the wills of these charming friends, now that our former cheerful home was filled with gloom.

No! no! it was far better for them to seek the sunshine, and green woods. But "Mouse" did not forget us. We were going down the lane—we told you about in the beginning—which led to the spring, where we found our pets, and we were greeted by familiar sounds. We turned hastily. There, on the fence, nearly down to the spring, stood "Mouse," looking so gay, so well, and so happy, and ringing out such a merry greeting, and hearty farewell, that we laughed with joy, and tried to forget all our sorrows.

THE JOLLY OLD CROW.

On the limb of an oak sat a jolly old crow,
And chatted away *with glee, with glee,*
As he saw the old farmer go out to sow;
And he cried, "It is all *for me—for me.*

"Look, look, how he scatters his seeds around,
He is wonderful kind to *the poor—the poor;*
If he'd empty it down on a pile on the ground,
I could find it much better *I'm sure—I'm sure!*

"I've learned all the tricks of this wonderful man.
Who has such a regard for *the crow—the crow,*
That he lays out his grounds in a regular plan,
And covers his corn in *a row—a row!*

"He must have a very great fancy for me;
He tries to entrap me *enough—enough;*
But I measure his distance as well as he,
And when he comes near, *I'm off—I'm off!*"

THE FAIRY IN THE WOOD.

ONE day as Mr. W. returned to the house he said, "I have seen a fairy, and know where she lives! But shall not tell anybody. If any one wants to know a fairy, he must seek her himself!"

In spite of all my entreaties, Mr. W. would not tell me what the fairy's name was, or give me any further intelligence than this. If I went to the squirrel tree, went up the wood-path over the hill, sixty paces, to a fallen tree, turned off fifteen paces to an upright stick, and then followed a trail ten paces more, it would lead to the fairy's house.

I determined to find it, and the next afternoon set out. It was my first lesson in woodcraft, and

Mr. W. was determined not to help me ; but walked after me, laughing and assuring me that the fairy did not disclose her secret to everybody.

At a squirrel tree we paused. I must think all the route out first ; and after I had fixed the direction in my mind I started, Mr. W. still following, laughing. The sixty paces carefully marked off, found me at the fallen tree, on the hill by the wood-path. Turning to the left, after twice returning to the tree, the fifteen paces brought me to the upright stick, which Mr. W. had planted.

There I halted. Now came the difficulty. What was the trail made of? Sticks, perhaps, or leaves, or—I could not tell what. I turned round and looked at Mr. W. He stood in the centre of the path, watching me with a quizzical expression. This was enough. I would not fail now! My eyes glanced round over the ground, then I began to scan every object—suddenly my eye caught a slender stem, pointing in an oblique direction ahead of me. I stepped forward and followed the trail, as I thought it.

It seemed to extend in a perfect line, but to my chagrin, at the end of it I saw no fairy's house or fairy! I retraced my steps without looking at Mr. W. I counted, and found it too long, and then came back to the upright stick. I turned round and round—crossed the path, and looked—no trail!

I stopped to think. I almost despaired, but it would never do to give up. Suddenly my eye fell upon a piece of wood—a mossy branch, around which no leaves were clustered, no spears of grass were bending over it, only a twig lying across it!

Ah, ha! and catching the idea, my eye wandered over the ground. I saw it all. Eight feet distant, a long branch lay across the roots of a tree, and it was in a line with this mossy branch, which I now divined did not belong where it lay.

I hurried forward; as I reached the end of the long branch, Mr. W. called out as he sprang forward, "Stop! stop!"

I stopped. I had discovered the fairy!

Sure enough, I had discovered the fairy! In the shadow of large tree-trunks, nine or ten steps in advance of us, vanishing with fleet glide into the tangle of stems and dead leaves which covered all the floor of the woods, her little feet making a light patter, like the hesitating fall of rain drops in summer nights that seek the thirsty wild flowers, at the base of grim, gray, mossy rocks, her eye gleaming soft and beseechingly at us, as she turned her brown-bared head—uttering no sound from her lovely throat, but departing silently, as if she meant to test our magnanimity, flitting away toward her lord in the forest, our fairy was gone.

We paused; Mr. W. pointed toward a little mound on the ground, so naturally thrown up above the surrounding twigs and dry leaves, that I could not see it even then, until he took a stick and almost touched it.

"There," said Mr. W. "our fairy keeps her jewels." I wanted sadly to get a peep at them, but the entreaty of our fairy's glance had touched my heart. I could not summon courage to gratify my curiosity, at the risk of having the jewel-box and jewels vanish. No ; I determined to bide my time patiently—in a few days, a week at most, the gentle fairy would, perhaps, permit us to gaze at her treasure !

So, with whispering voices and careful steps, we retreated from the enchanted ground ! We almost trembled when we thought—how can this wee fairy be secure against the intrusive visits of dogs, cats, raccoons, snakes, opossums, squirrels, and all the other creatures which gambol, prowl, or hunt over the face of the forest ? What if some huge spider should spring with sudden hunger out of his deep hole in the ground, and with greedy eyes spy out the fairy's castle—stretch out his long hairy legs, and with agile plunge settle himself amid her treasures !

Think of a spider among pearls ! or, panting beneath the surface of the black earth-mould, twisting himself like a gimlet, while the dirt sifts upward ; what if a goblin, gray and speckled, with face too human, and terribly ugly, with wrinkled, broad eyelids, flapping up and down over brilliant goggle-eyes, and with two long, bony, skinny hands placed next his sides, the palms outward and the fingers pointing nervously upward, as if to ask pardon for his extreme hideousness—what, I say, if this monster, this new-born toad, should, with unceremonious awkwardness, jump into her casket?

Think of a toad in a fairy's cradle!

But we must away, or we should become obnoxious also. What claim had we to linger near her? No, we must away! her little heart was, no doubt, anxiously throbbing, lest her faith in our generosity was thrown away! Her bright eye filling with tremulous light some dim shade, while she watched for our departure, Her ear was bending earthward to catch the last sound our heavy feet should make. We must away! We must tread daintily, for fear the clangor of our gigantic stride and footfall should scare away the wee fairy.

The tenth day from that we determined should be the time for our next visit. By that time, we thought, we shall have made up our minds to be very cruel—we knew that if we shrank, if our hearts grew tender, we should never even get a peep at that little fairy woman's treasures, much less be able to possess one or more of them.

Accordingly, each day we talked about what we meant to do; how we should manage—at what hour our visit was to made, and so on.

The tenth day arrived. The afternoon was clear and warm. But Mr. W. was in no hurry. The sun went slowly down: the shadows grew longer and darker; presently the blue haze in the distance became gray and purple and red, as the sun went below the horizon—and now all the shadows spread themselves over the broad bosom of the earth, mantling it like a vail, drawn over the aged neck of some century-old grand-dame.

A minute or two all was silent—and then, as long white lines of moonlight penetrated the forest, rose the mingled chirp of field-crickets, tree-frogs, and cicada. Then we sallied forth. Slowly we traced our way across the farm. Softly we stepped —lowly we whispered. Here we halted—in the hollow, where the elders grow by the fence.

Mr. W. carefully selects a long slender stem, and, testing its elasticity and strength, asked for my green vail. This I had in my basket, and gave it to him, and watched with connoisseuring air while he adjusted it at the point of the stick. Then we both tried what could be done with it for our purpose.

Mr. W. with cautious step advanced a little and endeavored to capture a clump of grass, but failed, and then handed the net to me. Softly, slowly I approached a group of field flowers, and lo! I had them safely netted!

"So much for a woman!" said Mr. W. "But you will not have the nerve to do the same thing at the castle of our fairy, I fear."

I shook my head in the negative. I was quite sure of that besides; my eyes were not so well able to penetrate the shadows, and I felt sure that our scheme would fail if *I* attempted to "net a fairy" in the dark. However, after a few trials, Mr. W. became perfect in throwing the net.

Arrived in the woods, we took a short cut across to the brow of the hill, some sixty steps from the door of madame the fairy's castle. Here we halted. Mr. W. laid down his powder-flask and shot-bag, gave me his gun—gave me his hat, which I laid on the ground with my shawl and basket. Then removing his shoes from his feet, and taking the elder pole with the green vail net at the end of it, with a gesture to me which signified " keep silent," he retreated up the wood-path.

In the mean time, the shadows had gathered blackness, until within the wood where we were, the trees stood solemnly in the stillness, lighted only at distant intervals by the cold, white rays of moonlight which struggled through, blinking and hesitating. Far over head, with a fierce red glare, one star was visible through the branches.

All was still. I had quietly seated myself upon the ground, bending forward to watch the retreating dim figure of Mr. W., who was now scarcely visible in the distance and darkness. In a moment more his form was hidden from my view entirely by an intervening trunk.

I listened! Not a sound could I hear. A minute passed! Suddenly, in a clear whisper, I heard my name called. I sprang forward, and glided with instinctive quiet into the shadows through which he had disappeared. I met him in a moment returning toward me, and could see through the falling glimmerings of the moonlight through the leaves that he carried something with the jealous care with which a treasure-seeker would bear the strange secret which he had found.

I whispered — "What! what have you done? Did you catch *her?* Did the vail answer?" He replied in a low whisper, as if for fear the old sentinel-trees around might hear—

"No, I did not—the trick of the vail and pole did not answer. Tread as softly as I might, the dried leaves and twigs would still be crisp beneath my guarded tread."

"Well, what have you here? what have you here?"

"O, step into the moonlight and see! The fairy *would* flit, and I have not her, at least. O, I feel sad that we must do such things! She went away like the flit of a moonbeam—so still, so soft, so gliding! I thought I could see her gentle eyes through all the shadows, looking with meek reproach, as if to say: O savage monster! how came you here to rob me of my treasure?"

And then, as we stepped into the opening of the road, and the broad moon came down in a pale, white sheet of silver, I saw he held in his hand a quaintly shaped nest, such as I had never seen before, covered with brown leaves, and arched over like some fairy grotto, lined with delicate and moss-like roots, and the soft fibres of thin barks. I peered into this strange nest, and—O wonder! what think you?—the fairy pearls had changed to little callow birds! I said, "Why could you take them—are they not too young?"

"I fear they are; but when I found the capture of the mother impossible, I did not choose to risk the loss of this little goblin family, when I had spent years and years searching for such a nest, and all without success until now. For they are so acute in hiding their dainty domicils, and frequent such still and shadowy places, with such dreamy, gliding movement, that they are almost impalpable actualities to naturalists."

It is an event to find the nest of the ground thrush; you might tramp on one a thousand times without knowing it in your heavy stalkings through the sere leaves of forests, without ever seeing or recognizing her—the mother—and with a perfect ignorance of her existence; unless you happened to be cognizant of the fact, that when a weary, lost and sweating wanderer, you sat down upon a stump or fallen tree, in the heavy forest, with every thing like thickets and shadow about you, you heard a low and sweet, soft song that did not aspire in its notes to be heard among the tree-tops, but which was only meant, like the cricket's chirrup by the hearth, to be heard as an undertone to inspire even the underbrush of nature with a plaining harmony.

O! how do we overlook so many of these quaint and musical things! Is the world always to be sonorous with the screams of eagles from its cliffs and tree-tops! Is mankind always to be overborne by cruel strength? Are we always to forget that there is an undertone of nature, and that its most mysterious music is, will be, and has been, always spoken in its "underbrush," where fairy people most frequent?

We took the little gaping, dim-eyed birdlings home with us, and gave them a house in a basket, tucked in with warm, soft silks and woolens, their cradle; and they soon became very intimate with "Mother Brush," and also with our three pet wrens, "Bob," "Mouse," and "Lady"—or rather, the latter became well acquainted with these babies, after having plunged themselves without ceremony into their nest, displacing their little fat bodies, to make warm nestling places at the bottom of the nest for themselves to take naps in.

But we have told you about the wrens, and some day we will tell you more about these children of the faries. At present, all we can say is, that we never saw more ambitious little creatures. They would run out of the nest before their feathers were half grown, every time they saw the "Brush," and such droll-looking scamps as they were—their chief beauty consisting in the fact that their mouths were as beautiful as wild flowers, and their breath fragrant as ripe nuts just fallen from the trees.

Just at this time we had a great deal to do—so many nests to see to every day. Over the other side of the brook we had a red bird's nest, a cat bird's nest, a yellow breasted warbler's nest, an indigo bird's nest, beside several others. Up on the hill lived a blue bird in a stump, and in the wood, where our faries lived, were our song-thrushes ; in the brier-field, just beyond this wood, lived a thrasher, who never hesitated to give me a beating when I went too close to her nest. A partridge had a nest in the ground, with an arbor of grass and twigs built over it, under a bush. Sly thing ! she did not know that we knew all about her secret.

Then down by the spring, where the raccoons came of nights, were several other nests. In fact, we had as much as we could attend to, watching the ways and oddities of all this large family.

But our family diminished ; by what means we could not for some time imagine. Sometimes we thought the little darkies were keeping watch on all our motions, and were in the habit of following us to steal our birds' nests. At other times we thought that the sheep or hogs destroyed them ; but then, if they did interfere, the nests would all be broken down—but no ! in almost every instance the nest was merely careened over, and the eggs or young carefully abstracted, leaving no trace besides this.

At length, one day, passing through the brier-field, we were attracted by the cries of a pair of ground sparrows. The poor things were flying back and forth, twittering and screaming apparently in great distress. Something was the matter! we stepped hurriedly forward.

"Stop! stop!" At that moment I cried out, Mr. W. lifted his rifle and fired! The head of a large black snake fell to the ground, while in the very act of making a spring at us. The ugly reptile had destroyed the young of these sparrows, and we now realized the meaning of the tipped-over nests. The snake had, without mercy, either penetrated the bottoms of the nests or had dexterously elevated himself above the edge of the nest and carefully taken out its contents.

THE GROUND SPARROW AND SNAKE.

Sometimes the birds quarrel fiercely for their homes and treasures, and quite often Master Snake

birds are not quite as tame as the animals. Even the hen and the duck does not liked to be touched by us. They will stay about our barn-yards, and feed from our hands, running after for food and water ; but they are very shy of being handled, and rather difficult to be caught.

The *dove*, or *pigeon* lives in houses which we provide for him, and comes even to our doors to be fed, but he don't like to trust himself in our hands. He is very timid and suspicious when any one approaches him, and will sooner lose his breakfast or his dinner than run any risk of being caught ; and they are most afraid of man. You will see them often in the barn-yards, and in the streets, running about among the cows or the horses, and under their very feet to pick up their food, without any fear, though they will fly away at once if a man or a boy stops to look at them.

The wild pigeons of the forest are of the same race, but they never come near the dwellings of men, if they can avoid it. They live in the deep woods, and make their nests among the branches.

The dove is one of the most beautiful of birds, though so common that he is not much thought of for his beauty. His form is the perfection of bird-like beauty, and his motions are very graceful. Their plumage is of various colors, but always soft and delicate ; and the neck is so glossy and brilliant in its covering, and so changeable in its hues as it turns from side to side ; the eyes are so soft and expressive, so quick and tremulous in their movements, that one cannot look at them without admiration and love.

Doves are sometimes kept in cages, but they do not like it. They prefer to live together in large families, and to have the free range of the air and the fields to gather their food. They are not polygamists—they live faithfully together in pairs, though there may be hundreds of them in one small house. Each pair has its separate nest, which they never mistake.

The dove does not sing, but has a very soft, plaintive subdued note, without much compass of variety, which is called *cooing*. It seems to be formed within, as if it came from the heart, and not from the throat, and is understood to be only an expression of affection for its mate. It sometimes has a very mournful tone, as if it were the dirge of a lost love, or a desolated family. The notes of some species are very sweet as well as plaintive. This is especially so with the *Zenaida dove*, which is found in some of the West India Islands. It is related of a pirate, whose resort was in the wilds of one of these islands, that he was so affected by the notes of this dove, that he was completely overcome, and resolved at once to abandon his wicked course of life. There was a reproachful tenderness, a soft pleading in the cooing of this dove that went right to his heart and melted it, like the voice of a mother's love. He yielded to its influence, escaped from the haunts of vice and crime, and became a man again, and useful member of society.

The *Ring dove* is very beautiful. It is a native of Europe, and takes its name from a pretty white ring, or circle of white feathers around its slate-colored neck.

There is a pigeon found in Africa, with a very rich green plumage, and beautiful blue eyes; but the prettiest of all is said to be the crowned Goura, as it is called, of the East Indies. While beautiful in all other respects, it has a splendid tuft, or crown of feathers on its head.

But perhaps the most interesting and useful of the pigeon race, is the carrier-pigeon, sometimes by way of variety, called the messenger dove. The first dove mentioned in any book was a messenger dove, probably of this very species. He was employed by Noah, to go out from the ark, and ascertain if the earth was dry.

The carrier-pigeon is trained to carry letters and messages from place to place, and is very faithful to its trust. It flies with great rapidity, and always finds its way to the place to which it is directed with wonderful accuracy. Before the magnetic telegraph was established, they were very much employed in conveying important messages, which required great speed and secrecy. The telegraph has probably deprived them of their occupation. Many very interesting and romantic stories are told of the carrier, but we have no room for them here. They would fill a book by themselves.

THE BIRD CATCHER.

SOME little boys were once told they could catch a bird by dropping salt on his tail. The following lines were written on seeing them try the experiment:

Gently, gently yet, young stranger,
  Light of heart and light of heel!
Ere the bird perceives its danger,
  On it slyly steal.
Silence!—ah! your scheme is falling—
  No: pursue your pretty prey;
See, your shadow on the paling
  Startles it away!

Caution! now you're nearer creeping;
  Nearer yet—how still it seems!
Sure, the winged creature's sleeping,
  Wrapt in forest dreams!
Golden sights that bird is seeing—
  Nights of green, or mossy bough;
Not a thought it has of fleeing;
  Yes, you'll catch it now.

How your eyes begin to twinkle!
  Silence! and you'll scarcely fail.
Now stoop down, and softly sprinkle
  Salt upon his tail.
Yes, you have it in your tether,
  Never more to skim the skies:
Lodge the salt on that long feather—
  Ha! it flies! it flies!

Hear it—hark!—among the bushes,
Laughing at your idle lures!
Boy, the self-same feeling gushes
Through my heart and yours:
Baffled sportsman, childish mentor,
How have I been—hapless fault!—
Led, like you, my hopes to centre
On a grain of salt!

On what captures I've been counting,
Stooping here, and creeping there;
All to see my bright hope mounting
High into the air.
Thus have the children of all ages,
Seeing bliss before them fly,
Found their hearts but empty cages,
And their hopes—on high!

THE PARROT.

IT does not seem necessary to enter into a detailed description of a bird so generally known as the Parrot. The different species vary from the size of a swallow to that of a domestic fowl.

The parrot genus includes about one hundred and seventy known species, and are mostly confined to warm climates. They generally live together in families, and seldom wander to any considerable distance; these societies admit with difficulty a stranger among them, though they live in harmony with each other. They are fond of scratching each other's heads and necks, and when they roost, nestle as closely as possible together. Sometimes as many as thirty or forty are sleeping in the hollow of the same tree. There they sleep in perpendicular posture, clinging to the sides by their claws and bills.

The young shoots of various plants, tender buds, fruits, grains, and nuts, which they open with much adroitness to obtain the kernel, are the chief aliments which the parrots use when in a state of liberty. In a state of domestication they eat almost every thing that is offered to them. In the forests, which are their favorite retreats, the parrots assemble in troops, and cause much devastation by the vast quantity of food which they consume, not merely for their subsistence, but to gratify that mania for destruction for which, even in their domestic state, they are noted. The loud cries of these bands are heard a great way off, when they seek their last repast before the setting of the sun. By these cries the planter has timely warning to employ some means of preventing these hosts of destroyers from alighting on his newly sown fields, where, in a short time, they would not leave a vestige of grain.

Some species establish their nests in the summits of the highest trees. The nest is composed of small sticks and slender twigs, interlaced with as much art as solidity ; the rest, and this is by far the greater number, choose the trunks of hollow trees, they there amass dust, and arrange grass and the filaments of roots, dressing the interior with their own down. The female lays from two to four eggs, altogether white, and sits on them with great constancy, whilst the male keeps himself at a small distance from the nest, attending to all the wants of his mate.

We can not pass over the sort of education of

which parrots are susceptible. They learn to speak and can retain and repeat a tolerably long series of words. This is the result of a forced modification of the voice, to which they have been brought by the habit of hearing the same words or sounds frequently repeated; and which, by the instinct of imitation common to all animals, but perhaps more strongly developed in the parrot than in most others, they are able to retain.

www.ingramcontent.com/pod-product-compliance
Lightning Source LLC
LaVergne TN
LVHW011207110826
845150LV00006B/1349

* 9 7 8 1 4 2 5 5 1 8 8 3 7 *